QANON UNLOCKED: SECRETS FROM THE SOURCE

Inside Q's Mind: The Deeper Q's Hidden Secrets and Theories

MR. BABYLON

CONTENTS

Introduction	v
1. WHO IS Q? IS TRUMP RELATED? WHERE CAN I READ HIS MESSAGES?	1
2. HOW TO DECIPHER Q'S DROPS?	4
Learning the Lingo of The Chans	9
3. THE TENTACLES OF THE DEEP STATE	11
The Politically Purported Truth	11
Europeans Need to Dispose of The European Union	14
4. THE PEOPLE BEHIND THE DEEP STATE	16
5. THE EPSTEIN CASE AND HIS FAMOUS CONNECTIONS	20
6. THE STORM IS COMING: THE 2020'S DECADE	26
7. DONALD TRUMP - WILD CARD	33
Court Cases and Bankruptcies	35
Run for The White House	36
Hard Times and Dirty Tricks	36
Smear by Smut	37
8. SYMBOLISMS	39
9. MORE ON SYMBOLISM	48
Sacred Geometry	52
10. THE NEW WORLD ORDER TIMETABLE	54
11. IMMIGRATION, WITCH HUNTS AND HEALTH CARE	59
12. HOSTILE MIND TAKEOVER	64
Only One Conclusion	64
The Same Phrase	66
Too Many Questions	68
When Fear Bends Your Mind	68
Isolation and Brainwashing	69
Brainwashing in Advertising	70

13. JOHN F. KENNEDY'S ASSASSINATION 71

   Glossary 75

INTRODUCTION

For those of you who have heard of QAnon, but only have a vague idea of what it is really all about, I'll provide a brief overview here.

In short form, QAnon is a conspiracy theory that alleges a vast, worldwide scheme by Evil Doers in the USA and abroad, known collectively as "the Deep State," to do lots of really bad things and keep doing them. There may also be a larger purpose or end game here— establishing the "New World Order" or some such—but it's not very clear. In fact, it seems (not surprisingly, when you look into the specifics) that the advocates for this theory can't quite agree on what the specific agenda of the Evil Doers is, other than to keep being really, really bad.

Fighting against the cabal of Evil Doers is a pair of heroes. The first of these great champions is Q, aka QAnon. Ostensibly a high-ranking member of the Trump administration with a military intelligence background, this nameless, faceless individual provides information— sporadically—via what are known as "drops." These are just coded pieces of text, called "crumbs," which further must be deciphered in order to have any meaning at all. Doing this are self-appointed Q interpreters, known as "bakers," who take the crumbs and cook them into something with meaning. Well, theoretically.

INTRODUCTION

Aiding Q in his selfless fight, tooth and nail against the Deep State, is our second hero: Donald J. Trump. Yep! He of the 10 days of golf per month, and 4-6 hours of TV watching and tweeting per day. Apparently, running the country and taking down a viciously powerful global cabal of Evil Doers doesn't take much time at all. Well, he has assured us he is "really smart" and a "stable genius," so this must be the proof.

The Storm (or something to that effect: mass arrests, uprisings, imposition of martial law, etc.) has been announced as immanent by Q multiple times, but has yet to actually materialize. Which I would argue is a very good thing, since the dreams of Q-oids sound fascistic and totally un-American to many, yours truly included.

In the broader sense, take any and all crazy, totally irresponsible, scurrilous, slanderous, outrageous claims you've ever heard anyone ever make, jumble them all together, add in baby mills, Satanism and human sacrifice, and then attribute it all to liberals—yes, bleeding heart liberals—and you now have QAnon in a nutshell.

I mean, I freely subscribe to the "conspiracy theory" which says Democrats (aka liberals), as a group, are completely incompetent. It's about the only "conspiracy" this group is traditionally capable of being a part of. The recent results of the 2018 midterms notwithstanding, the modern Dem Party has a stunning track record of snatching defeat from the jaws of victory. Witness the election that not only gave us the Man-Baby, but which put the GOP in charge of entire regions of the nation.

In summary, QAnon is, at best, an extremely dubious set of outrageous, unproven, slanderous "proofs" which, by the very nature of their delivery, are open to interpretation. Further, because many of them are so vague and ambiguous, it is relatively easy to make them align with known events, thereby providing "proof" for those who don't think too hard or delve too deeply into how ridiculous it all is.

You've probably searched the Internet and haven't found a reliable source that can answer your questions. There is no need to look any further; here you will find answers to your questions, in an orderly manner, and for beginners who have no idea about QAnon.

INTRODUCTION

Do not wait any longer, and keep reading, here we will teach you everything you need to discover and follow Q posts, and how to learn to read them. Thanks to the simple structure of the book, you will see that it helps you little by little to understand more deeply everything that surrounds us, and to realize that not everything is what it seems. You will learn to look at yourself critically.

1
WHO IS Q? IS TRUMP RELATED? WHERE CAN I READ HIS MESSAGES?

The QAnon movement did not start out with a bang. In fact, you can say that it only started with whispers. These whispers were done online on an imageboard that was frequented by what society considers as outcasts. These people were the perfect audience for Q because they are not your typical reader. These people are used to hoaxes so they are not easily swayed by what can be considered as crazy ramblings from someone pretending to have access to information that even the vice president of the United States may not have. After spending some time in the fringes, the QAnon movement began to seep into the mainstream.

Q silently emerged from the recesses of 4chan. This is an imageboard website where users can post anonymously. 4chan is divided into different boards that have their own content type and guidelines. It is important to note that this English-language site has been linked to internet activism and is the birthplace of many subcultures such as alt-right, Anonymous, and Project Chanology. The users of 4chan are the ones responsible for the creation and popularization of memes like Pedobear, lolcats, and Rickrolling. These people have been described by The Guardian as "juvenile... brilliant... alarming".

Q's very first entry was posted under the "Mueller Investigation" thread. This was found on the board known as /pol/. This first entry was logged on October 28, 2017. Q proceeded to post on various threads before the emergence of a new thread – Breadcrumbs - Q Clearance Patriot.

Q has long since grown to be a huge phenomenon, not just in the US but all over the world. Millions of people wait for his breadcrumbs and hundreds diligently do their research in order to analyze and interpret what Q means. As of 2019, there are over a thousand articles written about QAnon and the movement. Most that are written about Q and his followers are hostile towards Q and the people who believe in his drops.

Some are dismissive and see the QAnon movement as conspiracy theorists who will grab at straws. Still, others believe in what Q has to say and devote themselves to spreading his words. They tweet and retweet his posts. They make video analysis on every breadcrumb so that anybody who is interested in learning about Q and his truths understands what is happening. They share these videos, blogs, and tweets on Facebook so that they can reach more people. The shares on social media are staggering. Conspiracy theory or not, nobody can deny that Q has touched and influenced millions of lives. And the person that Q may have helped the most is President Trump. Without Q's help, a lot of his supporters may have already given up on this seemingly clueless leader.

The Anon in the term "QAnon" refers to the individual Q, who remains anonymous to this day, and the countless nameless supporters of this individual. While a lot of alternate theories rise and fall in the world of 4Chan, QAnon managed to stay alive for nearly two years. Why is this? IS it because Q knew how to give his audience just enough to keep their interests? Or is because people are awake enough to see that the person at the other end knows his stuff, unlike other theorists?

Followers wait for Q's entries to be posted. They believe that Q is using the website to secretly keep the public abreast of President

Trump's masterplan in eliminating the members and the leaders of the Deep State. When people started questioning whether Q really existed and whether he was really an insider, he showed the readers proof that he was with the President on Air Force One by posting a blurry picture of a few islands. This coincided with Trump's trip to Asia.

What does Q post? He reveals top-secret details in clue form. Eventually, these clues were labeled as "breadcrumbs". It was the readers on 4Chan who became the "bakers" of Q – the ones who put together the "breadcrumbs" that was posted and turned it into a "dough". The breadcrumbs are very hard to interpret as they appear to be a cross between ransom note and poetry. As an example, look at what Q posted in June of 2018.

After the bakers studied the dropped crumbs, they put their own spin to it and post it on their individual accounts. They talk about it on Reddit. They post videos of their interpretation on YouTube. They share links of other bakers' analysis on Facebook. This is how the QAnon movement grew.

2
HOW TO DECIPHER Q'S DROPS?

Part of Q's mission involves the exposure of global corruption. Naturally, those who commit criminal acts would not want their deeds exposed. That makes Q an enemy of the rich and powerful, and a target for retaliation. As a potential target of powerful people, if he were wise, he would want to avoid being identified. One way to conceal your identity from corrupt people would be to post anonymously on the internet. People have been doing that for years on the internet message boards called 4chan and 8chan (sometimes called the chans).

Q initially posted on the 4chan load up named politically off base (once in a while called/pol/). That board was picked for some particular reasons. 4chan clients can stay unknown, which is the reason government representatives once in a while use it to drop data about open defilement. The board is frequented by PC nerds who are skilled at uniting information from articles, recordings, open records, and different sources. By day, mysterious clients (likewise called anons or autists) fill in as frameworks experts, coders, and game fashioners. Around evening time, they inquire about the pieces of information individuals drop, without the information on their managers, and without realizing who composed the posts they're examining. (The term autist, as utilized on message sheets like 4chan, doesn't derive that an individual has chemical imbalance. Rather, it's a slang term that depicts individuals with the capacity to be hyper focused as they process a lot of data).

Anons have inquired about posts from insight network insiders (both genuine and phony) for quite a long time. Individuals consistently demonstrate up on the chans professing to be a specialist from the CIA or another insight office. They'll profess to have insider data on an examination or anticipate the capture of a celebrated individual, and as a rule, they're never gotten notification from again. Their expectations only occasionally work out as expected on the grounds that a great many people professing to be insight insiders are fakes. Managing fakes has made the anons a bored parcel. They'll expect a heap of verification before they'll purchase your "insight insider" story. On the chans, a fake is additionally called a LARP (or Live Action Role Player). LARP shows that the culprit of the misrepresentation is simply showcasing a job.

Q has figured out how to persuade anons of his authenticity, yet prevailing press outlets haven't tried to disclose this to their pursuers. In the numerous articles they've composed attempting to ruin Q, journalists will in general depict anons as fierce and simple fanatics. (This has not been my experience; I've seen them as profoundly insightful and systematic. In spite of the fact that they can be enthusiastic about their convictions, the anons who follow Q don't underwrite brutality.) After a huge number of negative articles had been distributed about Q and the anons close to the finish of July 2018, one of the anons posted the accompanying message:

Mysterious • Jul 30 2018 ARTICLES ABOUT QWHY DO THEY NEVER ASK THE ANONS WHY they're HERE?REAL ANON'S are here as we follow the EVIDENCE (archived evident proof), we are building the reality of our HISTORY so we will uncover and disassemble the debasement that has PLAGUED our reality for millennia. I welcome any distribution to print this as an announcement of certainty from an ACTUAL ANON. we do not mention to YOU what to think or the way to FEEL a few theme. WE essentially burrow for

TRUTH and afterward PRESENT what we discover so it tends to be examined by our PEERS and further corroborated. the selection to understand what we've discovered, checked and introduced is completely up to YOU. Introducing us add a fashion to infer WE are a kind of faction, shows the planet how degenerate the MAINSTREAM MEDIA has become. WE aren't about brutality, disruption or control. WE are just giving FACT based data freed from charge to the planet .WWG1WGAFeel liberal to SHARE End

Q reacted to the anon:

National security laws confine the data government authorities can give to people in general. Ordered data is untouchable, however there is an abundance of significant data that is open source. Actually, open source data is essential to such an extent that in 2005, the Office of the Director of National Intelligence (ODNI) made the Director of National Intelligence Open Source Center (OSC). The OSC is entrusted with improving the accessibility of open sources to insight officials and other government authorities. Similarly, that the OSC gives non-arranged data to its customers, Q furnishes his pursuers with data that is openly accessible to people in general and which, whenever united and accurately deciphered, illustrates what might some way or another require characterized data to comprehend.

Q Can Be Difficult to Understand

Numerous individuals discover Q's posts astounding. There are various purposes behind that. The principal reason is that Q utilizes a strategy for guidance that is once in a while utilized today. In the second 50% of the fifth century BC, critics were instructors who utilized way of thinking and talk to engage, dazzle, or convince their crowd to acknowledge a perspective. The Greek savant Socrates utilized an alternate way to deal with educating. The Socratic strategy is a type of helpful contentious exchange between people. The exchanging posing and replying of inquiries is utilized to compel basic reasoning, the investigation of thoughts, and the assessment of fundamental presuppositions. The Socratic technique prompts speculation end; better theories develop by consistently recognizing and dispensing with frail ones or ones that lead to logical inconsistencies. Normally, a progression of inquiries is presented that are planned as trial of rationale and reality. These inquiries help an individual find their fundamental convictions about some subject and distinguish convictions that ought to be disposed of.

We live in a culture today where correspondents put down articles and account interviews passing on their comprehension of an offered subject to us. It's increasingly similar to a monolog; there is no discussion included. There is no assessment of fundamental convictions. There is no trying of rationale or examination of the authentic premise of explanations. We're required to acknowledge the realities as they are given to us by the moderator without addressing them. The moderator doesn't only let us know "the realities." They additionally relegate importance to the realities. Whoever appoints importance to data decides the open account regarding that matter. The media will in general decipher data such that bolsters an ideological conviction framework. In the event that you acknowledge an individual's introduction of realities, you're bound to acknowledge their ideological convictions.

As opposed to the model of the predominant press, Q utilizes the Socratic strategy. Utilizing questions, he'll look at our present convictions on a given subject. He'll inquire as to whether our conviction is legitimate, at that point drop indicates about realities we might not have revealed, and propose an elective theory. He may give a connect to

a report and urge us to accomplish more research. The data we need is freely accessible. We're allowed to lead our exploration in the manner we need. We're additionally allowed to decipher the data anyway we need. We should arrive at our own decisions since Q downplays his understandings. For some, individuals, investigating for themselves, having an independent mind, and believing their own decisions can make following Q troublesome. At the point when you're acclimated with somebody mentioning to you what to figure, thinking for yourself can be a difficult change.

In spite of the fact that Q has an ideological structure that is focused on opportunity and equity, he gives data in a way that can be deciphered anyway one picks. To be sure, a typical analysis of Q is that his messages don't give any genuine importance since they can be deciphered in for all intents and purposes any way possible. The way that we're allowed to decipher Q's data anyway we pick doesn't mean there are no set-in stone answers. Q set up an arrangement of correspondence where specialists can request intimations or post the discoveries of their examination and have hypotheses checked. Numerous individuals have gotten affirmation or help from Q basically by posting their work on Twitter. Q may affirm our hypothesis similar to the case in this arrangement of posts from December 22nd and 23rd, 2017.

Dec 22 2017

How did NK abruptly have scaled down nukes upon POTUS getting to work?

What was expressed during Hussein's term by offices?

How did NK unexpectedly get missile direction top?

What is influence?

Characterize prisoner.

Their last expectation!

Q

An anon inquired as to why the letter "I" was absent from "rocket" in the above post.

Mysterious • Dec 23 2017

Q posts missing letter "I" are markers?

Q reacted with a piece of information:

What rocket terminated today?

[i]

Message sent.

Q

An anon reacted, taking note of that SpaceX had as of late propelled its Falcon 9 rocket to convey a variety of satellites for Iridium Communications.

Mysterious

Iridium?

Q affirmed the missing letter "I" in his posts was a sign about the Iridium satellites and said future news would open more data.

Future news will open a greater amount of the message.

Missing [i] affirmed.

Q

Exploring the hints gave by Q is tedious work, yet I've discovered that doing my own examination, coming to an obvious conclusion, and arriving at my own decisions encourages me comprehend recorded and recent developments in a progressively complete manner.

LEARNING THE LINGO OF THE CHANS

Conversations on 4chan, 8chan, and 8kun are hosted on various subdomains called boards. Each board hosts discussions on a particular topic. The boards are run by volunteers (board volunteers or BVs) who create and moderate conversations (threads). Board volunteers are sometimes called bakers. The threads are called breads. When a baker creates a new thread, they're said to be "baking a bread." A single comment in a thread is called a crumb. Helpful information on a topic is called sauce. The term sauce is derived from the word "source." If a point is made that isn't common knowledge, others will naturally ask for the source (sauce) of the information.

Q first began posting on the 4chan board, politically incorrect (/pol/), on October 28th, 2017. One problem with /pol/ is the high amount of traffic it receives. Some users are interested in participating in open discussions and research but many users are trolls and shills. Trolls and shills aren't interested in fruitful discussions. They derail conversations with pointless objections and oppose whatever idea is being discussed. Some people are paid to do this. Q's posts on 4chan were swarmed by trolls and shills which made it difficult for serious discussions to take place. One month after Q began posting, his threads had drawn enough opposition that the decision was made to move to 8chan which receives less traffic. 8chan was used by people around the globe to communicate on whatever subjects they want. Some users live in countries where freedom of speech is severely restricted. Many people are shocked to see nudity when they first visit these message boards. Jim Watkins, the owner of 8chan and 8kun, is a free speech advocate. If content isn't explicitly illegal according to U.S. law, he allows it to be posted.

3
THE TENTACLES OF THE DEEP STATE

THE POLITICALLY PURPORTED TRUTH

That general society has gotten disappointed and careful about steady Armageddon media reports and news inclusion that hold fast to corporate plans, is an obtrusive modest representation of the truth — individuals see their reality changing and they need to comprehend what's going on, and why. They need to be educated, to along these lines set themselves up. They need the opportunity to settle on taught decisions, rather than being determined what to do by the very people and organizations that continually lie and trick, the very foundations at the base of all the tumult.

Even with MSM disinformation (CH 7 and 36), the site Final Wake Up Call is autonomous and keeps on conveying fundamental and convenient data. 650 We are appreciative for the contribution of up and coming editors, donors, volunteers, and pursuers' responses in assisting with completing this undertaking of truth dispersal. The input from our pursuers is a significant wellspring of consolation and inspiration for continuation. Shortening the tide of disinformation being siphoned out by ground-breaking and very much supported prevailing press, is a significant test.

The control of the US and of worldwide legislative issues by the wealthiest families on earth, is practiced in a fantastic, significant and surreptitious way. This control started in Europe and has had a progression which will be followed back to when the investors found it had been more productive to supply credits to governments than to destitute people (CH 2). These financial families and their docile recipients have gone to possess most vital organizations (CH 7) over the 2 centuries, during which era they need subtly and progressively sorted out themselves as controllers of governments worldwide and as mediators of war and harmony.

Except if individuals completely get this, they're going to be unable to know the real purposes behind the 2 universal wars and therefore the approaching arranged Third World War, a war that's practically bound to start as an outcome of the US endeavor – with the guide of the EU politburo (CH 40) - to seize and control Central Asia. the most answer is for the U.S. also, the EU to ease off – something the individuals of the USA, the EU, and therefore the whole world actually need, yet not the force elites.

Be that because it may, the us has given the planet two options: war to shield the US Dollar, as against working with the Eastern Alliance towards the execution of another Gold Standard.

In spite of, or even on account of the irate endeavors of the world's Machiavellian destroyers, humankind is awakening. there's huge advancement being made in uncovering the progressing fierce Gaza eradication, the mass disclosures of HAARP's climate controls, the phony heating mantra – as lately modified into the global climate change mantra, Chemtrails harming the air and other neo-logical attacks, the moderate murder of humankind through toxin bound antibodies, even as the weaponization of pharmaceuticals and pharmaceutical methodology, the grievous impacts of EMFs (Electro Magnetic Fields) from different sources, GMO food control, structural RTF reconnaissance and observing, and at the up front, the obviously phony, initiated worldwide wars and therefore the militarization of society on the loose.

Try to not let these detestable practices occur or proceed, and guard against clear challenges in belief system losing you course. There's nothing level about this playing field and therefore the MSM mass story is an amazingly persuading publicity apparatus, initiated by the force world class. Try to not attempt to hear it out. depend upon the astuteness of your heart, acumen of the mind, insight, and presence of mind. Begin counseling elective news sources. The Illuminati's just weapon is our assent, whereby we respect their falsehoods. Disinformation fills a couple of needs, the foremost treacherous of which is that the presentation of uncertainty into your ardent feelings with reference to reality with regards to what's clearly occurring before you. Saving the mass psyche in check is basic for the satisfaction of their mystery motivation. The conventions of Sion which they follow, clarify that the target of worldwide control are going to be cultivated by controlling how the open thinks, by observing what they see and hear; by making new clashes or renovating old requests; by spreading craving, destitution, and plague; and by alluring and diverting the young. "By all of those techniques, we'll so wear out the countries that they're going to be compelled to supply us global control," broadcast the Illuminati. Peruse the Protocols 651 to perceive what more is coming.

Today, an ever increasing number of individuals around the world are awakening to the recently developing reality, with the understanding that what has been instructed verifiably, mingled and what we have been raised to accept politically as the fact of the matter, is a simple case of through and through horse crap.

Patterns and surveys lately have reported this move in perspective cognizance, reliably demonstrating a developing doubt of governments in both the US and Europe and to a developing degree in numerous nations of the world. A survey from January this year found that about two out of three doubt their legislature and another survey from April 2014 demonstrates three out of four accept their lawmakers are degenerate. Last October Pew Research Center found out that more than four out of five don't confide in their own legislature at all or if nothing else more often than not, a close to unequaled elevated level in the estimation of government doubt.

EUROPEANS NEED TO DISPOSE OF THE EUROPEAN UNION

EU parliamentary decisions were a finished and articulate disappointment for the European Union, with the point of turning into "the following United States of Europe," a flooding reaction of the eager enemy of EU voters from all over Europe sent periphery components from both the left and right to Brussels, with the particular plan to dispose of the European Union for the last time.

The voters' fury was heard with respect to the stale economy of France, the grimness vigilant Greeks, uneasiness in Denmark, right to Britain. A solid push for Ireland to quit the EU is developing. Numerous inhabitants, particularly in southern Europe were the hardest-hit countries, with serious grimness measures being forced by the almighty Germany, which is being accused for the monetary discomfort.

Oil-rich Scotland has even started to lead the pack in a dissident development, looking for autonomy from Britain. Cataluña in Spain looked for and decided in favor of freedom that has been obstructed by the Madrid government. Pais Vasco (Basque Country) in northern Spain idem dito. - Many Europeans have communicated hatred for large governments, which they fault for their high joblessness and bombed approaches, which have been seen as deficient in meeting their confined needs. Past the US and Europe, more residents around the world are becoming progressively furious with their chosen authorities, understanding that the government officials' sole need is to serve the necessities of their oligarch manikin aces, rather than the requirements of their own kin.

Russia-Bashing

U.S. President Barack Obama's war against Russia isn't just making Russia collaborate all the more unequivocally with the different BRICS nations to break the U.S. dollar's rule as the worldwide hold cash, but on the other hand it's pushing Russian President Vladimir Putin's endorsement rating higher, with work numbers in Russia taking off week after week and an ever-developing pace of certainty of the Russian individuals in their own Government.

The Ukrainian system, introduced by the U.S, has deliberately closed off any entrance of legitimate 'news' media into Donetsk - the star Russian eastern part − along these lines removing all covering the phosphor-shelling slaughter. Anybody despite everything hanging tight for the 'news' media to advise them about this firebombing, will most likely need to hold up until everybody is dead, before they stir to reality with regards to these violations. Actually, nobody cares, on the grounds that the more it takes, the less significant the 'news' will be — by then it will be history. The wonder of whether the casualties will be depicted as thoughtful in the history books, relies upon which side at last composes the history books on this war.

The illuminati are Satanists. They don't cry tears over a huge number of individuals in south-eastern Ukraine who are either being killed, or, more than likely escaping into exile camps inside Russia, all purposefully executed by individuals that the west has prepared and is financing, while at the same time being brought under psyche control. All trained activities are executed by the mystery plan, as spread out in the Protocols. For everybody in the western world, the applied assents with respect to Russia are deplorable for the entire economy on the two sides, explicitly Russia and the EU.

4
THE PEOPLE BEHIND THE DEEP STATE

When Obama set up the Iran deal and sent them billions of dollars, I couldn't stand by and watch any more. He was selling out the country to sworn enemies, and no one was saying a thing.

"I'm going to do it, John. I have no choice. I guess I knew I would have to since that day Obama flew Air Force One low over Manhattan and frightened people with his new power. All these years of his lies and deceit, and Hillary's personal agenda, have run America down. I want to make my country great again, as it was when we were prosperous, proud, and respected. I have no choice."

"You won't see me or know me," he said. "I'll be at your rallies and listen to every speech, and so will Carolyn. The millions who attend your inauguration will include me and my family. And when you finally get to remove the traitors and as many bribed people as you can, I'll reclaim my family name and stand beside you."

I rode the escalator to the lobby of Trump Tower and announced my candidacy, going up against 16 so called Republican hopefuls, and for the first time in my life, not being sure I could win.

I wished it was John who was running. I wished his father had never been murdered. I wished that the American people had never elected Obama or considered Hillary a viable candidate.

I knew my conversations with John would have to end. As a candidate, all of my communications would be scrutinized and we couldn't risk exposing him.

He was right about my tax returns. One of the first battles was about my tax returns. I was thankful for the IRS audit that kept them out of the public eye. I didn't need or want questions about the little corporation named Barin.

It was a long and sometimes nasty campaign. Hillary's arrogance and belief that enough fraud was in place for her win, angered me and kept me going.

On Inauguration Day, I quietly looked for John among the millions, and during the State of the Union, I thought I felt him somewhere in the balcony.

I checked my followers on Twitter and wondered which one was him. Neither of us trusted social media enough to expose his name or presence in any form.

I visited the graves of his father and uncle and thought of Jackie's love for her children. Once or twice, I thought I saw his smile beneath a beard, and once or twice I thought a handshake was his. I always felt him near me, and as I proceeded to do what was right for America, the thought of him coming back gave me some of the strength to keep fighting for the people.

Suddenly, Twitter and Facebook came alive with threads from someone named Q. It was my son who alerted me to the tweets and information. Q and QAnon became immediately popular with so many who also followed me. His tweets were most often questioning with urgent messages to people to connect the dots, do the research, and find the answers.

When he began saying, "trust the plan," I knew John was somehow connected, and even I had to remember to trust the plan.

The media thought it was a hoax, and Twitter tried to shut him down, but I checked every day to see what was being said and how much people were learning. To do what was necessary to "drain the swamp," many people embedded in the agencies around me had to be arrested, indicted, and convicted. Hillary had to be marginalized or jailed, and the CIA and FBI had to be scrubbed.

It wasn't going to be a quick fix, and I knew I would be attacked from every side. When I needed to feel support for what I was doing, I scheduled a rally or a speech that would bring the energy of the people back to me.

Assassination attempts were rampant and my wife and son were being threatened daily, but I was alerted to all attempts by those around me who were loyal to the country, and also by the tweets from Q. He would say, "POTUS is safe," and I'd know the right people were there to protect me.

I forged ahead with the plan, running into obstruction everywhere, but still managing to slowly make the changes necessary. Obama's presidency had been a Coup d'état, many people not realizing that their country had been taken over or that we were in a war. I had to do what was right for the people, and what was right for America.

"When everything is in place, and only when it is, forge ahead."

John had managed to send a tweet without exposing himself, and I felt re-energized. When I met with Kim Jung Un, I knew it was right. And when Putin gave me a soccer ball and said the ball was now in my court, I was certain almost everything was in place.

Then, during a short press event about Russia, the lights went out for several seconds. When they came back on, I knew I had the full faith and support of everyone who would be involved in bringing America back, and I knew it wouldn't be long before I could shake the hand of the man who had helped me through it all.

Q, if you're out there and can hear me, we're ready and God is with us. The people are awakened. God bless America.

5
THE EPSTEIN CASE AND HIS FAMOUS CONNECTIONS

Allegations against Epstein

The first allegation against Jeffrey Epstein came in March 2005 when a woman informed the Palm Beach Police Department in Florida about an older girl taking her 14-year old stepdaughter to Epstein's mansion. The woman informed that her stepdaughter was offered $300 for stripping and massaging Epstein. The woman also stated that her daughter had apparently undressed although leaving Epstein's mansion wearing her underwear. Following the allegations, police started an undercover investigation of Epstein that spanned for 13 months. The FBI also participated in the investigation after a short gap.

Abuse of underage girls

The police subsequently uncovered evidence that allegedly tied up Epstein with payments to many girls for engaging in sexual acts with him. The concerns of Epstein abusing underage girls are evident in the interviews with alleged victims and the witnesses under oath as well as a high school transcript alongside certain items found in the trash and home of Epstein. The police correlated all these evidences to find out that almost all the girls who were sexually harassed by Jeffrey Epstein were under 18 years of age. Evidence also suggested that the youngest victim was 14 years old and the majority of the victims were under the age of 16 years. The police also came up with more substantiating evidence regarding the involvement of Epstein in abuse of underage girls upon searching his home. The police found two hidden cameras in Epstein's house along with many photos of girls all over the house. The police also found that some of the girls in the photos found in Epstein's house had been interviewed during their investigation process. According to statements of one of the former employees of Epstein, Epstein used to receive massages for at least three times a day. Finally, the FBI compiled a report stating that 34 minors were confirmed for their allegations of sexual abuse by Epstein and the proof was evident in corroborating details. The number of confirmed minors eligible for restitution, according to the FBI was increased to 40 in the non-prosecution agreement (NPA).

Pedophilia

Epstein was found to be involved in the abuse of underage girls through the police investigation. Also, he was also found to be involved in pedophilia according to investigations. The police chief at the time of the investigation, Michael Reiter, stated that there were over 50 girls and one boy who had allegations of sexual abuse by Jeffrey Epstein. However, the concerns of pedophilia came into concern when allegations of 12-year-old triplets brought in from France on the occasion of Epstein's birthday surfaced. Obviously, sexual abuse of underage girls can also be classified as pedophilia, but Epstein did not have any such boundaries. The 12-year-old triplets in question here were sexually abused and flown back to France the next day. The investigation findings also indicated that many underage girls were brought in from South America, Europe, and former Soviet Union countries. The Palm Beach police filed a probable cause affidavit in May 2006 which stated that Epstein should be charged with four counts of unlawful sex with minors as well as one instance of sexual abuse.

Famous Connections

In many of the victim and witness testimonies, one fact appears explicitly visible! What is that? Epstein escaped justice for quite a long time, and that is definitely a fact. Look at the treatment he received after being convicted as a sex offender and sentenced to 18 months in prison. Epstein was placed in a private wing of the Palm Beach County Stockade instead of the state prison that is the usual place where convicted sex offenders in Florida are housed. After three and a half months, he was allowed to leave jail for around 12 hours a day for 6 days a week on 'work release.' Epstein was released after 13 months of 'prison sentence' for a year of probation on house arrest. However, the 'house arrest' also allowed Epstein to take numerous trips to his residences in the US Virgin Islands and Manhattan. These events clearly suggest that Epstein was not just a man of money but also a man with some powerful contacts. Epstein had a spectacular list of friends belonging to the elite class of society. So, let us take note of some of the important names that have been associated prominently with Jeffrey Epstein. One important fact to keep in mind here is that a majority of Epstein's contacts denied any form of involvement with him after allegations of sexual abuse and trafficking on Epstein surfaced in 2005.

Bill Clinton

The contact of Epstein with former US President, Bill Clinton, is one of the hot topics currently on the table for journalists and conspiracy theorists following Epstein's death. Epstein visited the White House and supposedly met Bill Clinton for the first time at a donor event during the presidency of Bill Clinton. Epstein is reported to have had meetings with a White House aide many times. After the end of Bill Clinton's presidency in 2001, the contact between Epstein and Clinton grew stronger.

Clinton was in a new stage of his career and was driven to travel the world and launch many philanthropic activities. Clinton had to hang out with celebrities and rich people during this time and make huge sums of money. According to a 2002 New York magazine profile, Clinton was attracted to Epstein solely for his plane. Clinton's aide Doug Band mediated the meeting between Bill Clinton and Jeffrey Epstein. In September 2002, Epstein took Clinton along with actors Kevin Spacey and Chris Tucker on his private jet for a tour of five

African countries. Subsequently, Bill Clinton was also with Epstein on many other trips such as another trip to Africa, one to Asia and one to Europe. These statements are confirmed by the spokesperson for Clinton, Angel Urena. Clinton's team has also clarified in the past that Clinton's trips with Epstein were primarily about democratization, citizen service, fighting against HIV/AIDS and empowering the poor.

Clinton was accompanied by Secret Service agents and his security detail at all times on his flights with Epstein. Clinton's spokesperson clearly stated that the trips were meant to forward the work of Clinton Foundation. Bill Clinton had commented about Epstein to the New York Magazine through a spokesperson. Clinton stated that Epstein was a highly successful financier as well as a committed philanthropist. Clinton had also added that Epstein had a keen sense of global markets along with comprehensive knowledge about 21st-century science. One of the alleged victims of Epstein, Virginia Giuffre, also stated that she had seen Clinton on the Little St. James Island, the private island of Jeffrey Epstein. However, Giuffre also stated that she never had sexual relations with Clinton. She also added that she had never seen Clinton having sexual relations with anyone on the island. The spokesperson for Clinton, Angel Urena, stated that Clinton had never visited Epstein's ranch in New Mexico, his residence in Florida or his private island in Little St. James.

Prince Andrew

Another notable name that comes up frequently among the mentions of notable and influential friends of Epstein is the Duke of York, Prince Andrew. A report states that their friendship began in 1999 when they met each other through Ghislaine Maxwell, who is also a renowned British socialite. The relationship of Epstein with other members of the royal family is not known. However, Prince Andrew was photographed walking with Jeffrey Epstein in Central Park in 2010 after Epstein had finished his prison sentence. In a recent statement released on August 24, 2019, Prince Andrew has claimed that he stayed at many of the properties owned by Epstein. He also added that he did not meet with Epstein very often and saw him only once or twice in a year. Epstein has also been connected to Prince Andrew through the latter's ex-wide Sarah Ferguson. According to a report by the Telegraph in 2011, Epstein had paid £15,000 to the former personal assistant of Sarah Ferguson based on the orders of the Duke of York. The payment was supposedly responsible for a wider restructuring of Sarah's debts worth £5 million. Sarah Ferguson has apologized for her involvement with Epstein and has confirmed that she will repay the money and also stated that the payment was facilitated by her ex-husband, i.e., Prince Andrew.

Furthermore, unlike many other leaders who issued statements denying any form of involvement with Epstein, Prince Andrew did not speak anything on the matter for many weeks. However, recent statements were issued by the Buckingham Palace in August 2019 that was related to the relationship between Prince Andrew and Epstein. Prince Andrew also admitted recently that he had committed a mistake and an error by spending time with Epstein in 2010 even after his conviction as a sex offender.

The official statement by the Buckingham Palace also includes the statement of Prince Andrew in which he claims to have never seen, witnessed, or suspected any form of behavior that led to Epstein's arrest and conviction. The Buckingham Palace had published two official statements regarding Prince Andrew's involvement with Epstein. The most notable point of association between Prince Andrew and Epstein arises from the allegations of notable Epstein accuser, Virginia Giuffre. Giuffre claimed in court documents that she was forced to have sex with Prince Andrew at the age of 17 years by Epstein. She has also claimed that she had sex with Prince Andrew on three different occasions. Therefore, Prince Andrew appears to be another elite member in the network and friends of Epstein who denied contacts with him after his involvement in the sexual offense allegations.

Others

Epstein also had many other notable names in his network and his friend circle. One of the prominent names is the CEO of L Brands, Les Wexner. Epstein managed finances for Wexner and reportedly, he is the only listed client of Epstein's own financial consultancy firm.

Wexner actually purchased Even the Manhattan residence of Epstein in 1989 through a trust. After Wexner moved to Ohio with his wife, Abigail Koppel, in 1996, the ownership of the house was transferred to Epstein in 2011 for just $0. However, according to a recent statement by an L Brands spokesperson, Wexner had severed all contacts with Epstein after firing him from the position of finance manager over a decade ago.

The different names in Epstein's network have some sort of connection to Epstein at some or the other point. While the exact nature of the relationships between Epstein and his network of friends is not clear, mainstream media reports have associated Jeffrey Epstein with some top names in the world. Some of his notable contacts include Michael Jackson, Rupert Murdoch, Katie Couric, the Kennedys, the Rockefellers, Michael Bloomberg, the Rothschilds, Alec Baldwin, Kevin Spacey, Chris Tucker, Richard Branson, and Woody Allen among others. He also had friendly ties with Israeli prime minister Ehud Barak, British prime minister Tony Blair and the Saudi Arabian crown prince Mohammed Bin Salman. These names speak a lot about the type of power Epstein enjoyed during his lifetime.

6
THE STORM IS COMING: THE 2020'S DECADE

"The 'cabal' has owned the current banking system since before World War II." "Q" explained. "As such, all transactions must travel through 'cabal central' banks, where the 'cabal gray men' have the last 'say' over what will be done with the money. Over the last several decades, nothing happens in the banking business unless the 'gray men' approve it."

"So, if they control the 'money supply' as well as the destination, what chance do we have to take back our world?" Sheryl asked. "Even if we assassinate every last "cabal banker' in the world, they still control the 'system' itself. They control the SWIFT transfer systems. Right?"

"You are so right, my dear!" "Q" proclaimed. "Unless we can wrestle control of the SWIFT banking transfer system and its 'codes', we will never be able to overcome their power over our lives."

"Then what is the answer?" Rami asked. "You must have already figured this problem out? Right?"

"Yes," Caroline replied. "It has to do with a completely new banking control system which involves 'Quantum control banking', an 'A.I.' banking system. It will solve all the current banking problems, and together with the 'Manna World Holding Trust', a new world will be created."

"How in the world could we ever wrestle control from these people?" Sheryl asked. "It seems an impossible situation!"

"You are so correct." "Q" replied. "But that which is impossible for man is quite possible for God."

"God raises up the necessary "Master" from every realm of His Kingdom when they are needed the most." Caroline answered. "In this case, a miracle occurred which ultimately led to a takeover of the various Trusts themselves."

"Throughout time, "Q" explained, "the various 'Trusts' owned by the cabal, were officiated over by a single Trustee, who was responsible to transfer such funds to the locations requested by the Cabal leaders. As time passed, control passed to a very special 'agent' of the Almighty Creator; this woman is now simply known as 'Kim'; her formal name is 'Kim Gauguin', a 7th generation Rothschild!"

"Kim has turned out to be the actual savior of this planet," Caroline said. "She became sole Trustee in 2015, and immediately began to accumulate all the various Trusts into one giant trust, which is now described as the 'Manna World Holding Trust'. Kim has decided to refuse to use these funds on behalf of the Rothschild cabal."

"Instead," "Q" explained with great delight, "Kim has decided to use the giant Trust funds for the betterment of the human race. She has also taken the funds out of the 'SWIFT' system of banking, wherein the 'cabal bankers' would have continued to maintain control over the use of the funds. Instead Kim has chosen to use a new and improved 'Quantum A.I.' Aided banking system. No other person in the world has access to this money; Kim's action will lead directly to the bankruptcy of all the 'cabal central banks', including the 12 Federal Reserve Banks in the United States."

"Wow", Rami exclaimed. "That is the greatest news we have ever heard. Why is that we have never heard of such a thing?"

"Not many people understand how the banking systems works;" Caroline replied. "But this is a 'game-changer' for the world.

"So, we do not need to worry about the banking system?" Sheryl asked. "Without their access to money, what will the 'cabal' do to maintain their control?"

"They are still a powerful group," "Q" announced. "They still have their 'armies' in Europe (NATO), and they have their 'assassins', and their access to plenty of nuclear weapons.

"The U.S. new Quantum banking system will be handled by the Treasury Department, which will be centered in Reno, Nevada." Caroline added. "The Internal Revenue will be dismantled and their employees moved to the Treasure Department. The Federal Reserve assets will be taken over by the Treasure Department, and the 'cabal bankers' will be escorted out of the country."

"Kim has been a God-send", "Q" announced. "She will ultimately transfer appropriate moneys to every country in a fair honest manner, as she will do to the United States. Since our country will no longer be giving 'all' of our taxes to the 'cabal bankers', the United States will become a very wealthy country, and all 'income taxes' will be eliminated. Further, Kim will transfer 'trillions' of dollars to help America begin to rebuild our crumbling infrastructure. The future of the United States, as well as the world, has never been brighter."

"Wow" Rami exclaimed. "Now all we need to do is to eliminate the 'bad actors' in our government, business community, media and entertainment system. Have all of those individuals been identified?"

"Funny you should ask about that!" "Q" exclaimed. "That is what we will discuss right now."

"The President refused to deal with the Vatican money representative Cardinal Pell," Caroline explained. "All the money in the world would never convince Trump to make a 'deal with the devil'. As soon as he was elected, Trump decided to attack a number of 'dark players' in our nation. He started with those persons involved in the 'pedophile world' together with those involved in 'human trafficking'. It is this group who provide the young children and woman which the alien creatures need for their physical survival. In addition, the alien monsters taught their 'players' to also participate in their 'Luciferian' rituals, where children are tortured and killed, blood drained, and served as food to all in attendance. You may remember the 'discovered laptop' computer belonging to Representative Weiner; the information of the computer reveals in graphic detail the behavior of top Obama characters, included Hillary Clinton. President Trump has gone after the entire 'pedophile' community, which included many working in the entertainment and music industry. This 'pedophile' community also included many in government service, as well as many in the media and the 'social network' business. Trump will not rest until all of these 'scum' are arrested and sent to prison."

"Yes, I did hear about all of this," Rami announced. "But I was not sure whether all of that was real of just 'fake news'."

"It is very real." "Q" replied. "As of this moment, the following 'big names' who have been indicted include 'former' President George H.W. Bush, who was executed by a military tribunal. His son, George Bush, was also indicted and will soon be executed by the same military tribunals located at the Gitmo U.S. Base in Cuba."

"Are you suggesting that two former American Presidents were arrested and found guilty of 'capital offenses'?" Sheryl asked. "What were their crimes?"

"Both were indicted for their involvement in the death of my father, John F. Kennedy, as well as the attempted assassination of Ronald Reagan." "Q" explained. Those facts are exactly what brought about the attempt on my own life a few years ago, as we discussed earlier."

"Alright" "Q" replied. "let's get back to business."

"OK, we were talking about the 'bad actors' in our government." Caroline explained. "let me give the names of a few other criminals who worked for our government. We identified two former Presidents who were indicted, but there will be at least two other American Presidents who will be indicted. Also, indictments are forthcoming for those involved in the 'Uranium One' deal, as well as the 'Clinton Foundation' problems. Further, as of this date, there have been eighteen (18) attempted assassinations of President Trump. Our organization always knows in advance when these attempts are going to arise, and to date, the President has survived each attempt."

"My God," Rami adds. "The Democrats want him dead this badly?

"Most of these attempts come from the 'cabal' itself." Caroline replied. "But there are a number of Democrats who have also been involved. All of those involved will be indicted, and in a short time, more than eighty (80) members of the Senate and House will be indicted, mostly Democratic members. But the 'cabal's' reach also includes Republicans. In addition to the Bush family, indictments will reach people like Chaney, John McCain (executed for treason), Vice President Pence (trafficking), Donald Rumsfield, Romney (offshore taxes)."

"You do remember the eight-year Presidency of Obama. A lot of strange things occurred, including the 'Uranium One' deal, as well as Obama's Iran settlement deal. Caroline continued. "The military was not very happy with the behavior of the Administration during the Obama years. It was during this time that ISIS grew from a small 'J.V. Team' into a very power and wealthy terrorist group, taking authority over vast areas in Iraq as well as Syria. The Administration also cut funding to the Military to dangerous levels, which eventually brought the military leadership to consider intervening to stop the direction and future safety of the United States."

"When you say 'intervention'," Sheryl asked "are you talking about a possible 'coup' of the American government?"

"Yes," "Q" replied. "In fact, a small group of military intelligence officers decided that they had no other choice but to remove Obama from his position. This group formed a committee which is today call the "Q" group. I am a part of that group."

"But I assume that your group did not seriously consider 'coup-d-tat'", Sheryl asked. "Please tell me that such an idea did not take effect?"

"No," "Q" replied. "Instead, the ten of us on the "Q" committee decided to see if we could locate a candidate who could actually win the election against the presumed Democratic candidate, Hillary Clinton. We created a list to ten people, took a vote, which narrowed the list to two people, Donald Trump and Ted Cruz. We first approached Trump, who immediately agreed to run for President. Trumps only question was as follows: if elected, do I have to 'do what you ask'? We replied, 'No, just do what you think is right. That is all we ask'."

"So, did you engineer the election of 'Trump'? Rami asked.

"Yes, we did." "Q" answered. "You see, the previous Presidential elections were not really 'free elections'. The 'deep state' had control of a 'quantum computer' which was located underneath the Denver airport. Each election, going all the way back to the Bush/Gore Presidential election, was controlled by the 'quantum computer' controlled by the 'deep state'. In fact, the 'deep state' elected George H.W. Bush, Bill Clinton, George Bush, Hussein Obama and were prepared to elect Hillary Clinton in 2016."

"So how did your organization disable the 'quantum computer'?" Sheryl asked.

"We used their own trick against them." "Q" announced. "We took away their computer's abilities half-way through the night of the election, and then used our own 'quantum computer' to insure the election of Donald Trump. So, when we say that Donald Trust was 'selected', and not 'elected', we mean what we say!"

"I do not believe what you are saying?" Sheryl added. "Are you certain of what you say?"

"This is God's truth." Caroline replied. "We just did to the 'deep state' what they had been doing to American over the last twenty-eight years."

"Oh My God!" Sheryl cried out. "I do not know what to say"

"We did what was necessary to save not only this world, but to save the entire world." Caroline replied. "We are working on three major problems in this world: the alien problem, the 'cabal/pedophile' problem, the 'banking problem, and the problem involving 'free elections' in the U.S.A."

7
DONALD TRUMP - WILD CARD

Now we come to December 23, 2016, the date on which President Obama signed into law the updated National Defense Authorization Act.

Aside from funding the military and extending the provision that allows for arrest and incarceration without trial of anyone "suspected" of being associated with terrorism, something else was added but buried deep inside the legislation - the "Countering Disinformation and Propaganda Act."

The irony of this is that the US has for many decades engaged in its own form of disinformation and propaganda, both domestically and internationally, through outlets such as Voice of America, National Public Radio, the New York Times, the Washington Post and most if not all of the mainstream (fake stream) media.

It is another sign that the "gray men" are doing everything they possibly can to hold on to the reins of power - even though those reins are slipping through their fingers at an accelerating pace.

There is a policy in the establishment media of not reporting the many assassination threats that are made against the president, although they do mention the occasional event when it suits their agenda – their agenda being, in the case of Donald Trump, character assassination.

Independent assessments have shown that since Donald Trump's election, the mainstream media coverage has been up to 97 per cent negative.

That's why the mainstream media front has been filled with a constant barrage of fake news about Russia having hacked into the Democratic National Committee files and released emails to Wikileaks, which in turn supposedly released them on the Internet, which in turn (the mainstream media would have us believe) influenced the election campaign in favor of Donald Trump.

There's another way to look at this though, and that is, instead of seeing a conspiracy involving Russia and the Trump campaign, how about a conspiracy involving puppets of the gray men within both parties, in all of the US intelligence agencies, and the mainstream media – a conspiracy to discredit or obstruct the new president in every possible way.

You may recall the media reports that Trump was briefed by intelligence agencies which expressed what they called "a high degree of confidence" that Russia did what they say Russia did. And yet, they have also admitted that there is no way to say exactly how Russia's "interference" actually affected the election results.

Nor did they offer any specific proof at all that Russia was responsible for any hacking. They just claimed to have "a high degree of confidence," which really means nothing at all without facts and real evidence to back it up.

It was all a deliberate ploy.

With the puppet media and puppet journalists staying focused on the "Russia did it" meme, along with their "everyone else is fake news" claims – while they themselves propagate all the fake news they can make up about Russia – anything to do with the revelations in those emails about the Clinton Foundation or Clinton Charities or about an active pedophile and child-trafficking ring and other horrendous activities is effectively off the radar.

Such is the art of perception management by politicians, bureaucrats and the media.

They want us all to hate the president, and they're doing it using one of their assassination techniques. It's called character assassination.

Instead of getting sucked into their agenda, shouldn't we be thinking for ourselves, and asking ourselves, just who is this new president?

Before we get to a prophecy Ramtha made about President Donald Trump meeting UFOs, it would be prudent to look at the background of this man who is now the 45th president of the United States.

Now that he has shocked the gray men to the core by winning the election despite all the negative publicity, the manipulation of voting in the primaries, and the regular character assassination "leaks" that occurred, the new president is in the White House, and it looks like he's determined to stay.

As for his background, here's a shorthand version gleaned from the public record.

COURT CASES AND BANKRUPTCIES

Around 500 bodies of evidence against Trump were excused. He won multiple times, lost 38 - and the consequences of the rest are hazy to the extent the open record goes.

While his rivals have intentionally suggested that Trump has been a bankrupt, he has never by and by petitioned for financial protection. Or maybe, his lodging and club organizations have been pronounced bankrupt multiple times, however that was done intentionally so as to re-arrange obligation with banks and proprietors of stock and bonds.

RUN FOR THE WHITE HOUSE

Over the years, Mr. Trump considered running for various political offices, but it wasn't until June 16, 2015, two days after his 69th birthday, by which time he was worth over $4 billion, that he announced his candidacy for the 2016 presidential election.

Trump paid much of the expenses of his campaign from his own fortune, and he now donates his presidential salary to various causes. He works as president for $1 a year.

HARD TIMES AND DIRTY TRICKS

The New York Times, which throughout the campaign was clearly biased against Trump.

Dirty tricks from a biased media have always been part of the election process, but the same goes for politicians themselves - they resort to every underhanded trick they can think of in their efforts to win votes

Project Veritas, which produced a series of short election-related YouTube videos using under-cover methods, revealed that Clinton campaign insiders were deliberately setting up confrontational protests, including the use of clowns, and planning to bus Democrat voter's interstate to boost her vote and poll numbers.

Although they would deny that they had any intention of influencing voters, publications like Politico, The Washington Post, The New York Times, and the Los Angeles Times all took pleasure in running anti-Trump articles. All of them would claim they were simply pointing out what they termed as lies or falsehoods in Trump's campaign statements.

If that was true of Trump, it was equally true of the Clintons.

A record 84 million people watched the first debate between Donald Trump and Hillary Clinton, after which Trump's opponents went into overdrive, leaking a tape of Trump making lewd comments about women - for which he later apologized.

Trump responded in one of the next debates by telling an inconvenient truth - that Bill Clinton had not just made lewd comments about women. Trump said Bill Clinton had actually 'abused women' and that Hillary had "bullied her husband's victims."

Bill Clinton, he said, "was impeached and lost his license to practice law and paid an $850,000 fine to one of the women, Paula Jones."

Those who wish to split hairs, as attorneys and some journalists tend to do, point out that the $850,000 was not a fine, as Trump claimed, but a settlement, without Bill Clinton admitting liability as to the charge - which was one of harassment in that he (Clinton) had exposed himself to Jones in a hotel room in 1991.

The way the US electoral system is set up, the final decision on who gets to be president is made by what's known as the Electoral College. While Hillary Clinton won the popular vote (and there are questions about whether that was achieved by devious means), Trump won the decisive Electoral College vote.

That was an absolute shock to the Globalists who had done everything they could to ensure that Hillary Clinton would be elected.

Nevertheless, she and her political machine were not about to go quietly. Instead, they were planning every conceivable way to discredit and destroy the man who had thrown a monkey wrench into their Globalist plans.

That was when the Democrats and their allies in high places came up with the "Russia Interfered" and "Russia and Trump" smear campaign.

SMEAR BY SMUT

Something very strange happened just prior to the inauguration, and here again we may sense the presence of the gray men and their puppets. In early January, Trump was briefed by top intelligence agency officials, including the then head of the CIA, on allegations that Russia had "potentially compromising personal and financial information" about him.

A private intelligence dossier was later leaked to the media and to the public containing the claims. Some of the material alleged dubious sexual and financial conduct by Trump, and reporter Bob Woodward called the unsubstantiated dossier a "garbage document" meriting an apology from whoever wrote and leaked it.

Keep in mind that character assassination is one of the tools of politicians everywhere, but it has proven particularly useful in the past for the Globalist/New World Order people who have been very careful about putting their own followers into positions of power, and not just as politicians, prime ministers or presidents. Many of them are the people who make up The Deep State, being in positions of power within various government departments where they usually have long-term tenure.

Many of them can be found within the media and government agencies, especially the intelligence community.

Leaking that totally unsubstantiated document with all its salacious lies and the ensuing media frenzy no doubt harmed Trump's image in the eyes and minds of many, which it was intended to do.

And then came the inauguration.

But first, let's look at two incidents involving President Trump and UFOs.

8
SYMBOLISMS

This title and statement first appeared in Q post #184, repeated to some degree in several later posts (i.e., Q post #1002 "Symbolism will be their downfall."), and refers to the use of both historically occult and "domestic" symbols by Elite members of political groups, religious and scientific organizations, financial and academic institutions, and even powerful royal families. Specifically mentioned in post #184 are the icons of the "owl" and the letter "Y", although quite different in literal appearance, they do connect in occult ways not readily perceived. However, symbolism in general and even in regards to these Elite - often at the center of conspiratorial global agendas - is not limited to these two listed here and as such I will outline three categories of symbols one might encounter when reading the Q drops.

Symbols, most often represented throughout history as (but certainly not limited to) geometric patterns, usually in conjunction with numerical or mathematical significance, are used for a variety of purposes. They may be used as "identifiers" to signal like-minded individuals or to communicate ideas and concepts when words alone cannot. On occasion, symbols used in a magickal or ritual setting can be utilized in a way that heightens the emotions and focuses the intent of the practitioner. (As a side note, magick or magickal is purposefully spelled with a "k" in order to differentiate from regular stage magic. This alteration of the word is commonly attributed to the infamous early 20th century occultist Aliester Crowley but is widely used by many people for the same reason given.) These types of symbols, such as the "Y" mentioned in the Q post above, range from the simply positioned (though quite complex in its philosophical and spiritual implications) Christian cross to the elaborately designed sigils of the Keys of Solomon - see and compare the images shown below:

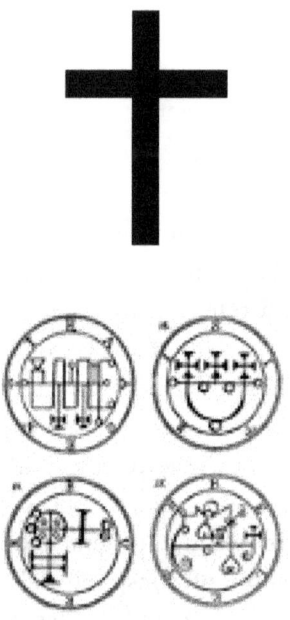

One may also encounter symbols of a "physical" nature or of a seemingly mundane characteristic, but even so, this does not reduce the power or meaning of the symbol. For the sake of simplicity and to appeal to the understanding of those unfamiliar with such concepts, I will use the widely known mythological Bible tale of Adam and Eve as an example. (Another side note - myths are often regarded as "fictional" accounts or just silly stories that our ancestors told to explain why the sun comes up, but in fact are deep narratives which convey a greater truth about ourselves.) In this story, Eve is tempted by the snake to eat the "apple" or fruit from the Tree of Knowledge. The apple here is the physical or mundane object and is symbolic of the concept of the Knowledge of Good and Evil, which in itself is a symbolic aspect of the Tree. This action of consuming the apple of course leads to the ousting of Adam and Eve from the Garden of Eden. (see figure below)

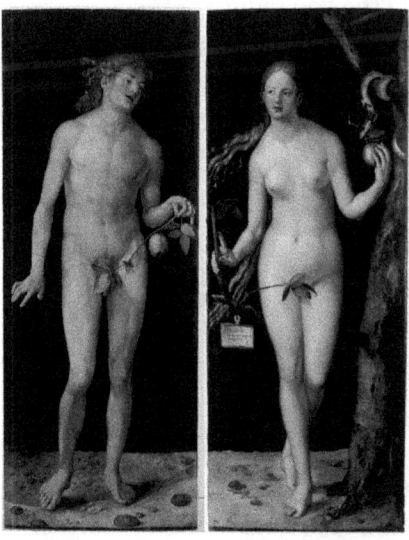

While the apple is a very general and generic example of "physical object" occult symbolism, there remains a "domestic" or "contemporary" subcategory of this type. Without exploring this subject in great detail, as there are numerous other resources for those interested, an excellent example (although quite malevolent in implication according to released law enforcement memos) would be the coded imagery of pizza originally gleaned from certain leaked emails and pertaining to a certain unnamed restaurant. Pizza is a "domestic" type of symbolism as it has only existed in relatively modern times and is encountered by the population on an everyday "mundane" manner. However, this "pizza" example can also be represented by the type of geometrical patterns previously described, and are not limited to a modern interpretation. The first image below is a direct correlation that one can make between the implied meanings of "pizza" and this geometric representation put out by law enforcement.

Alternatively, while not exactly the same, similar images have appeared throughout history and have held different meanings not necessarily attributed to the dark and perverse context as some people have implied in relation to the previously mentioned emails. For example, we can see a relation with this triangular spiral image with the valknut of Norse origin and the god Odin.

This symbol of three interlocking triangles was, according to Ellis Davidson in the book Gods and Myths of Northern Europe,

One could speculate, although loosely and probably falsely, that the "binding" power and meaning was carried forward (either intentionally or unintentionally) and applied to the modern pizza-spiral symbol without having any direct relation to Norse mythology. I will state here that it is not my belief or intention to promote any real connection between the ancient and modern symbols, only to point out that (just like information) symbols are not in and of themselves positive or negative. It is only until placed within an individual's framework of intention do, they take on one or more of those perceived qualities. A skull-and-crossbones image can have a negative impact as pirates (or a secret society) attempt to loot and kill their targets or it can have a resulting positive result appearing on a bottle of poison, preventing someone from drinking the toxic substance and saving their life.

Third, and lastly, of the symbolic categories covered here are those of archetypes. Primarily attributed to depth-psychologist Carl Jung for originally coining the term, archetypes are often the most complex of symbols as they encompass multiple levels of meaning, appearance, and description mostly in relation to the human psyche. They not only manifest as characters in stories and myths but they quite often appear in more subtle areas like dreams. Many archetypes have qualities that tend to hit a "primal nerve" and the concepts that are related to them can be felt regardless of one's culture, creed, location, or generation in which they lived. However, one can also experience personal archetypes aside from or in addition to those existing in humanity's mass subconscious mind.

Let us again examine the previous mythological example of the story of Adam and Eve, although I am only translating this in the most elementary way in hoping that readers can begin with at least the most accessible understanding. In this story appears the third character of the serpent, which is perhaps one of the most ancient and long-standing archetypes among the human race. (see figure below)

Throughout history and across the globe, the image of the snake or serpent has held many meanings but quite often, as seen in the Garden of Eden story as the animal symbol of Satan or Lucifer, those in Western cultures have a deep underlying notion of aversion, fear, or even revilement without even consciously thinking about it. Part of this, as I tend to think, is merely because of our cultural programming and thus becomes evident in our encounters with real physical snakes. The other part of this reaction, though, seems in some way inherent of genetic or ancestral memory and thus is actually a natural reaction for people even without exposure to theological belief systems. In contrast to this, there are images of the serpent which represent entirely alternate meanings. From the Egyptians and Greeks comes the symbol (and, according to psychologist Carl Jung, who coined the archetype term) of the Ourobouros - a cosmic serpent eating its own tail relaying the cycles of existence - later adopted by alchemists and magicians. (see figure below)

While there is nothing overtly sinister about the symbolism of this serpent, one can imagine or pull from one's subconscious a possible feeling of fear in relation to the contemplation of one's own mortality. It could also be fear of the unknown, fear of self-destruction, or any number of other negative attributes that one could imply. In this way, the possibility exists to link one symbolic representation to another (i.e., the Serpent of Eden) with an underlying psychological effect while having no actual significant contextual connection. This is the primary function of the archetype as symbol.

Please take a moment to remember the "owl" mentioned in Q post #184. The owl is, for many, aside from its form being a traditional cultural symbol, also an archetype in its own right. (See image below)

The owl can embody so much and can personally contain so much meaning that it would be impossible to devote even several books about it. Although Q is most likely referencing here a certain statue of an ancient god and an Elite ritual called the Cremation of Care, (see image below)

I suggest that the reader think deeply about the context of owl symbolism in one's own life and what it means in contrast to Q's post. If the reader feels adventurous on this specific archetype (from a QAnon 40,000 ft. advantage), I would suggest investigating a book called The Messengers: Owls, Synchronicity and the UFO Abductee by Mike Clelland although this has no correlation to QAnon - merely an interesting rabbit hole which to travel down.

The mention of the owl in Q post #184, as previously mentioned, also has a strictly aesthetic connection to the "Y" as an incarnation of the ancient god Moloch only in an implied way: The symbol of "Y" is representative of the "bull" or "horned oxen" characteristics of Moloch and is mentioned in the Bible numerous times (as well as other sources like John Milton's Paradise Lost) and has a deep association with the act of child sacrifice, often associated with some of the rituals allegedly performed by members of politically powerful secret societies. This is how we connect the deity of Moloch to the statue of the owl, though no religious or historical evidence exists. Moloch imagery is also manifested in the symbolism of the Minotaur from Greek mythology as the creature who dwelt in the Labyrinth and feasted upon humans. I shall explore this specific tangent at a later point in the book.

There are other categories of symbols such as omens, but from my viewpoint they are not directly relative to the QAnon information drops, whilst also remembering that the three of which I have mention are mainly conveyed by Q through written text on the internet. Mythology, as a whole, incorporates iterations of all types of symbolism in story form. By becoming properly acquainted with how symbolism can potentially impact an individual and the framework in which symbols might appear, one can gain a degree of insight into the subliminal motives, activities, or beliefs of public figures and groups being scrutinized. Through the use of symbols one can also attain a deeper understanding for the gain of one's own knowledge and understanding or to see things from a different angle that may be more beneficial for a given purpose. In light of the three categories all symbolism (and the deep contemplation of them) give the reader a wider outlook when digging for information and how to apply it. I will not be fully analyzing the entire QAnon posts referenced, and instead leave it to the reader to try for themselves. Don't forget - "Expand your thinking" and "question everything" and you just might discover something that brings your mind closer to a state of freedom.

9
MORE ON SYMBOLISM

In late 2014, Apple, Inc. became the first company to be valued at over $700 billion, making it the most valuable company in the history of mankind. And their logo just happens to be a single image that corrals and encompasses exactly the Great Plan? Of mankind seeking knowledge (technology) along the path to becoming an immortal?

Pardon the pun, but was Apple picked to be one of the torchbearers for the Great Plan of advancing man's technological capabilities? Or were they marked for success because they were inviting in otherworldly help with their occult symbol?

Whether the founders of Apple intended it or not, Satan and his demonic host are attracted to symbols that can call upon and welcome their interference in our world. This is exactly why symbols are used in Satanic ceremonies, such as the pentagram and hexagram. They are virtually a 'seal of approval' from the humans that the evil ones have our permission to come and interact with whoever is presenting those symbols.

By Apple, Inc. using the particular symbol they did, they arguably attracted the attention of Satan himself to take that company with that exact logo for the Great Plan and advance them to the top, which is exactly what happened.

How about the #2 most valuable company in the history of mankind, Exxon.

'Exxon' the name contains the symbol of Satan himself in it as you will soon see here. Another coincidence? How about Microsoft? Do you see that Internet Explorer logo on your screen? The one that is a representation of Saturn once you fill in all the blue on the 'e'? Occult symbology is all over the biggest corporations in the world and it's exactly because they are trying to enlist the help of the supernatural.

Symbols are all around us all the time no matter where we are, and they certainly get our attention. Symbols give direction to those who know what they represent. The occult symbols we're going to go over are more than just shapes to be sure. They originated in mankind's ancient history and give directions to the operatives of the New World Order.

I had reservations about sharing with you what we're going to go over because you're never going to be able to look around you the same way ever again, especially the symbol of the Christian cross. The cross is the globally-accepted symbol for Christianity to those who don't know what it really represents.

Unfortunately, the symbol of the cross not only originated in the occult, but it originated as exactly a Satanic symbol. Just like the holidays are truly Satanic, paying homage to the Antichrist King Nimrod and by default Satan, the cross is originally a symbol for Nimrod and Nimrod-reborn on December 25 as Tammuz. The cross was originally called a Tau, named after Tammuz. In ancient Babylon. Just because people believe it represents Jesus does not make it so any more than believing that Christmas is really about Jesus and not the Antichrist. This all goes back to what Jesus told us about loving God with our minds, not our eyes. This is exactly why God forbids any images of anything Divine in the Ten Commandments.

We have been under a constant deception ever since we got here on Earth around 4000 BC, and very, very few have been able to see through this deception, understand it, and warn others exactly what is going on. This is precisely what the prophets did for God back in the day. That's what the Bible is: God's 'called' people telling His followers exactly what's going on, even if it's bad news they just don't want to hear or abide by, let alone accept as bare-bones truth.

How many times did God's prophets call out the ancient Israelis and Judahites for straying, calling them 'a rebellious people'? It seems, as a whole, they were on the naughty list more often than not in the Bible. They were only rebellious in God's eyes though, as all the societies around them had been mired in the Satanic Matrix forever, and they were just joining the crowd basically. When the ancient Israelis strayed, it was just over to the side of 'general society' at the time.

It seems that most of our fellow brethren are in this exact spot today: Following the Satanic holidays, displaying the Satanic symbols, worshipping on Satanically-designated days, chasing money, fame, power. etc. Most of the brethren seem to only step out of the Satanic Matrix for one hour, one day a week…….and it's on the wrong day.

Now, the only way the Great Plan can work is if a small, secretive group of people are controlling it. Not everybody can be the boss on this planet; you need bosses who give direction and workers who execute it. In today's world, the Illuminati are happy to assume the boss role, but they have to prove they are worthy to Satan himself and that's where the occult symbols and ceremonies come in.

When the Great Plan got up and running again in ancient Sumer after the Flood, the proponents of the Great Plan needed occult symbols in order to network. These ancient symbols meant different things to different people. The meanings of the symbols were different to the occultists as opposed to the general population. Satan's people understood the exoteric meaning and the esoteric meaning, but the public-at-large were only meant to understand the exoteric meaning, which is whatever they were told it meant at the time. The exoteric meaning changes from empire to empire, but the original esoteric meaning never changes. This is why they recycle the same symbols over and over. The meaning only changes for the deceived, never for the deceivers.

This is why today people are calling the 'Star of Rephan/Saturn' the 'Star of David'. Most people have no idea the hexagram is representative of Satan himself.

Symbols are hugely important to the people running the Great Plan. They didn't have smart phones back then, so they needed to be able to communicate with each other secretly but have their message out where other occultists could see it and know that whatever it was attached to was part of the plan, the Great Plan.

Well my friend, there's not really a 'correct' order to what we're going to go over, other than I tried to categorize the occult symbolism world the best I could. Truly the only way to be considered an 'expert' on the symbolism we're going to go over is to be an insider to the operations of the Illuminati, which I am obviously not.

I think I did a well enough job to get you at least pointed in the right direction. There is such a vast body of information about the New World Order it can be overwhelming and it was before I got saved and everything came into focus. We're just beginning to ramp up a supernatural battle of Biblical proportions and most people don't know the magnitude of what's happening and what's coming just yet, but you certainly do and will know even more as we go forward together in my works.

It is possible that there are even more meanings for the symbols we're going to check, or maybe a debate about my interpretation of one or more. All of it. Anything at all. I welcome open discussion about anything and everything I'm talking about. We're all adults here, this certainly isn't a kid's book. There is nothing in this book people should be afraid to talk about because it's all based on the truthful facts as always.

God wants the people who actively seek it to know the truth about the very things we're talking about, and that is why you are here with me right now, at this point, in this book:

You seek the truth.

SACRED GEOMETRY

Sacred geometry is all around us, all the time. These are the geometric shapes and patterns that our 3D world is constructed of. The very reason geometry is 'sacred' to the occultists is that these shapes and assemblies of shapes originated from the Divine blueprint of how our world operates.

Sacred geometry is found everywhere in our existence, from going from a thought to physical form as a bee makes a honeycomb from perfect hexagons, from a snowflake which always manifests as a hexagonal/6-sided shape, all the way to the very building blocks of life at the subatomic level, which again are typically 6-sided in shape.

The ancients have left us a plethora of evidence that those running the New World Order way back then knew of sacred geometry and put it in designs on everything, from symbols such as the Seed/Fruit/Tree of life to the symbols of the pentagram, hexagram, etc. that are used in black magic/occult rituals.

Not only did the ancient occultists know things that the general population is just now finding out through advancements in science, but by them being shown how to hack into God's natural system by Satan/Azazel and the Watchers way back in the pre-Flood days, they were and are able to obtain even more occult information, prognosis of the future even in my opinion. It's just like they're hacking into God's computer network, with the ways to do this having been passed down over the millennia by the ever-regenerating proponents of the Great Plan. Those ways are exactly the gruesome Satanic blood and sex rituals they perform in honor of their god, Satan.

Sacred geometry has been incorporated into the designs of religious structures of all walks of life, buildings, towns and even entire cities.

One look at the street map of Washington D.C. and it's not hard to see that it's laid out according to the occult and many have already made the case showing that it is in fact laid out incorporating occult sacred geometry. Virtually every significant federal building in Washington DC has a Masonic plaque on it, from Washington Monument to the George Washington Memorial, so this should not be a surprise at all around Capitoline Hill.

Sacred geometry has been turned into religious symbols of all types, appearing on religious structures, art, stained glass, amulets, necklaces, bracelets, rings, clothes, and all the rest of it. In other words, it's everywhere you turn and always has been……just like the followers of Satan.

10
THE NEW WORLD ORDER TIMETABLE

The New World Order of the global elites are preparing for themselves underground cities stocked with food, water, ammunition, medication, and other provisions to survive a future life changing event upon the surface of the earth. These underground military facilities are being built secretly in the United States, Israel, England, Russia, Norway, etc. It has been estimated there are at least 150 underground bases in the USA. A selected elite will be residing in these facilities, during a devastating global catastrophe. The bankers in Frankfurt, Germany are constructing bunker sanctuaries. Elite CEOS are purchasing properties in remote areas of the world away from coastlines. Conspiracy theorists claim they are aggressively promoting their smart green technologies, based on the premise of global warming, leading to a cashless society, a one world government, and a microchipped population. Everyone and everything will be reliant on the electric grid through the use of RFID and biometric technologies. Their UN Agenda 21/ 2030 plan of sustainable development, is an agenda of removing personal liberties, such as private ownership of vehicles, property, and guns, where all must recognize the needs of the collective, not the individual, for the common good for a one world government to be implemented by 2030.

These global elites are an occult secret society known as the Illuminati, or referred to as The New World Order. These thirteen bloodline families are all powerful and influential, their wealth and assets accumulated, more than the combined funds of the world. Their members are the most powerful bankers, financiers, celebrities, politicians, and business people that are exclusive to the Bilderberg Group, and the House of Windsor and the Vatican are also included. Their plan of domination of the world is currently unfolding, as they manipulate the world's economies, markets, fund both sides of the wars, control the mainstream media, and work towards 24/7 surveillance of everyone using the technology of RFID chips, and Biometrics. Their quest is for a one world government, religion, cashless society, and the reduction of the world's population level to a sustainable 500 million people, in a world of slightly over 7 billion.

The global elites hold high level positions in key corporations and institutions. Their decisions are consequential to the fate of every human being, and the civilization of the world. They are devoid of moral or ethical principles, their secrecy is the essence of their power, and never risking disclosure. Their agenda includes distraction, and deception, to maintain control of the masses, for they fear uncontrolled societal chaos, a potential threat to their plans for the human race. They have their contingency plans in place, while the population will be the last to know, and the first to perish, while they believe they will remain protected.

Their secret occultist doctrine teaches that the ancient peoples worshiped gods and deities, that traveled to earth, from a planet star known as Sirius. The Egyptians acknowledged this star, as Anubis, the jackal headed God. A statue of Anubis is displayed at the Denver International Airport, as well as other mysterious paintings, and a time capsule. It is believed by conspiracy theorists that the Denver International Airport is the new headquarters for The New World Order. The pagan religions of Babylon, Egypt, and the Sumerian, were based on myths that described reptilian ancient astronauts that visited earth, and mated with women, being worshiped by mankind as gods and or goddesses.

The elites know the future, know what is coming, and have constructed massive protected underground facilities, to sustain their lives for a considerable amount of time. Their observatories and highly powered telescopes give them unlimited access to astronomical and scientific data that we the public are not privy to. Since they control the mainstream media, they keep any credible information from leaking out, debunk any whistle blowers or truth seekers and promote false propaganda. Due to the numerous Nibiru arrival prediction dates that have been proven false; this only helps them persuade the public to ignore the warnings about Planet X. It is believed that scientists and researchers, have discovered the path of Nibiru, and the discoveries have been suppressed, by mysterious disappearances or death, due to their knowledge of this ultimate cover up deception. They know that this crisis will usher in economic and social upheaval, and have made plans to invoke martial law, and set up Fema detention camps for this purpose. If no danger exists to the earth, then why the need for extensive preparations and a cover up of them?

The NOAA has determined that nearly half the population resides in coastal areas. Our Federal government has covertly moved our national capital resources from Washington, D.C. to Denver, Colorado where it is reported the construction of vast underground facilities now exist there, for the headquarters of the New World Order. In addition, the New York Federal Branch of the Federal Reserve has moved its headquarters to Chicago. Danger zones would be the east and west coastlines of North America, South and central England, and big cities, and low-lying areas. Through the use of geoengineering HAARP weather modification programs, they perpetuate the mass deception concept of global warming. Apparently, planned military operations, such as Operation Indigo Sky fold, spray toxic and biological agents in the atmosphere to cover up any evidence of Nibiru in the sky. Pilots are briefed that it is a strategy exercise to combat greenhouse gases and global warming. They create chemtrails in the sky to prevent any visibility of approaching Planet X, with this black op mission.

According to unnamed sources in military intelligence, our public health officials have been preparing for a cataclysmic disaster. Hospitals are storing large provisional supplies such as gas masks, medicine, and body bags. The government has been stockpiling food, ammunition, medication, and water supplies over a period of years. There have been many drills and contingencies for large scale disasters, and a national emergency alert system available on every cell phone that has been established. FEMA who serves the NWO elite will be in charge of dividing the country into zones, after the catastrophe, and implementing martial law. Silence is another tactic that is used by the global elites, as they control the mainstream media and Hollywood, only what they want reported on, will be told, perpetuating their ideals for public consumption. The Illuminati are ruthless and twisted in their ideology, as they feel the rules do not apply to them, because they have the power to make the rules. In their code, they believe that before their enemy is destroyed, they must have a chance to be forewarned through symbolism or clues, so they can have a fighting chance.

Thus, conspiracy theorists believe they use the Hollywood movies of today to suggest dark futures for the planet, invoking occult images, Egyptian myths and symbols, and global disasters. These promoting interplanetary creators of mankind, such as Star Wars, where humans and aliens co-exist with robots or droids., and space travel between planets is common. The force is portrayed as an energy field representing all living things binding the galaxy together. There is the light force for good, the Jedi, and the dark force for evil, the Sith. In Star Trek, Gene Roddenberry, the creator of the series was a 33rd degree Scottish freemason. One masonic symbol is their pyramid shaped communicators, Spock's masonic V sign, and the United Federation seal of planets is very similar to the United Nations seal today. The movie Stargate in 1994, was a sci-fi adventure that led to a planet with humans that resembled ancient Egyptians who worshiped the god RA, with pyramids and this ancient ruler. Deep Impact premiered in 1998, with the storyline of a comet that threatens the earth, unless it can be destroyed, and only those allowed into shelters will survive. The movie 2012, reveals a plot of world leaders that make secret preparations for the survival of the select elite of society to be sheltered on a gigantic ark, while a series of global catastrophes threaten to annihilate mankind. In the premiere of the movie, The Mummy in 2017, a betrayed Egyptian princess that has been entombed under the desert for thousands of years is unearthed, once she is resurrected, she goes on a monstrous rampage. The NWO use occult imagery, hand signals, and place subliminal messages in videos and songs. Prominent hand signals are the hidden eye, all seeing eye, devil's horns, the pyramid sign, and the V sign. The highest levels of freemasonry are devil worship, and covert Satanic religion. Biblical prophecy links the New World Order to Luciferian Freemasonry, whom are under control of the Antichrist.

II

IMMIGRATION, WITCH HUNTS AND HEALTH CARE

Can we make a better tomorrow, a better future for our children? Of course, we can! The question is not really whether we are able, but whether we are willing. As things stand and look at present the answer to the question of whether we are willing seems to be a resounding "No!". There are simply too many people that are not in the least bit interested in changing, much less learning to understand those with differing views and then accepting them as they are. So many are genuinely afraid that if they allow themselves to accept differences and be tolerant of them that they will somehow be betraying their own beliefs and/or views. They are afraid that if they show compassion and tolerance then things will run amok, as if things aren't bad now with them stubbornly clinging to their intolerance and therefore helping to perpetuate the problems we see today. They seem to fear that showing compassion, trying to be more understanding and display tolerance is equivalent to weakness. Take the very hot topic of immigrants and immigration. People, politicians... even entire states are doing everything in their power to try to run immigrants out of the country and also make it impossible for the ones who stay to gain legal citizenship. If you look at it very carefully, you can see it for what it is. Racism and fear. Racism because all the new laws and legislation are designed specifically to target Hispanics, and in particular Mexicans, without outright saying so (to avoid being seen for what it really is). This country was founded by nothing but immigrants! I hear the term "American" so often used in the sense of a race of people, and often added is that in order to be a "good American", one has to hold some very specific views such as America is the only free country in the world, guns are almost equal in status to the Bible, Christianity is (or should be) the official religion of the State, and English is the only language worth speaking. As the joke goes, if you speak three languages you are trilingual. If you speak two languages you a bilingual but if you can only speak one, you are American.

During a recent televised golf tournament, a family member remarked, "OK, we can leave now. At least I know an American is going to win." It wasn't said with a tone of simple patriotism, but rather with a distinct distaste for any other nationality. But back to the immigration issue. States are passing laws that make it very hard for anyone who doesn't have white skin. These laws, regardless of what their proponents claim, are not aimed at, say, Russians or someone from the U.K. No, they are plainly targeting Mexicans. Do these people not understand that we need these immigrants? After all, with unemployment so high, white people are not flocking to the fields to work all day, every day, in the blazing sun, for very little pay and no benefits whatsoever. It's not just in the fields either. There are many jobs that Mexicans do that white people simply refuse to do because it's too hard, pays too little or they simply see the work as somehow beneath them. If all the immigrants (meaning here Mexicans) left as so many of the "good Americans" want them to this country would be in serious trouble. Food prices would skyrocket because nobody would be willing to work in the fields without far more pay than immigrants receive, nor would they do it without insurance and benefits.

That's just one of the areas this country would be in trouble with. As with my statements about politics and politicians, this is simply fact and there is no need to argue it because it is self-evident. Almost everything we use and purchase would skyrocket in price. Not just food, but let's look at what would happen in the fields. Farmers would be forced to pay at least legal minimum wage (that's right, immigrants don't even get that) and provide safer working environments. Immigrants are exploited because it's easy to do so. They are undocumented so what are they going to do, what government agency are they going to complain to? The people who hire them know this. Please don't misunderstand me, I am not at all saying that immigrants should be exploited, I am simply pointing out the fact that they are. They are exploited and looked down upon. And they make an excellent scapegoat for politicians. Blame all crime on immigrants and you have yet another bogeyman for white Americans to be afraid of. After all, it seems we Americans need "others" to be afraid of and blame all our problems on. We don't like taking responsibility for our problems. So, we have our new witch hunts... Mexicans and Muslims. We want to, as evidenced through our entertainment (films, TV, books), news media and politicians, blame all our problems on "others". Blaming virtually all crime, not to mention our economic problems of our own doing, on immigration is simply too convenient. The same with blaming all the world's problems on Islam and Muslims.

Not long ago it was learned that the FBI had been teaching its agents that mainstream American Muslims were most likely all terrorist sympathizers and that Muhammad was a cult leader and nothing more. That's right, the FBI was actually having a class teaching its agents this load of nonsense. The FBI now claims it has stopped the nonsensical "training", and if they actually have, I'm sure it was because of their being caught in such nonsense and not because of their own moral compass. Now police in Arizona and other places are free to racially profile anyone of Hispanic heritage. With all my pointing out these uncomfortable facts, you may think that I am Hispanic or Muslim (or perhaps both) and therefore have some personal or cultural agenda for pointing these things out, but I am neither. I am simply stating the facts, ugly as they are. I also find it odd that, considering our crumbling infrastructure in this country, we can find and spend billions on perpetual wars but seem utterly incapable of repairing/maintaining bridges and roads. We could go a long way toward easing, if not outright ending, hunger not only in our country but around the globe if we put the money, we spend on killing into feeding. And yes, there are people right here in America who go without adequate food, shelter and medical care for those of you who may not be aware of it. The "American Dream" has become a sad joke. Even for those lucky enough to have jobs right now, our society is set up, seemingly designed, to use people up and then discard them. For example, a person is expected to go to public schooling, graduate and get a job (don't forget getting married and having two children), belong to some church, work at that job sitting in that cubicle (or slaving away in the sun), be placed on anti-depressants, anti-anxiety pills (and don't forget the cholesterol lowering drugs), have a heart attack anyway, retire (if you live long enough) and then try to have enough money to cover all your prescription drugs, food, medical costs and then if you are still alive, be placed in an "assisted living" facility and then finally die. Does that really sound like your idea of a "dream"? To me it sounds like a nightmare! I suggest researching, or better yet (for anyone who can afford it these days) France and the lifestyle of the French or those of other developed European countries. Here is a short list of some of the things European visitors to America notice right away:

Not as many people walk or use bicycles

Everyone looks tired

How big everything is, particularly vehicles (as one noted, "SUVs everywhere!")

Everyone is in a hurry (I'd like to address this one further later)

All the disposable things, particularly cups and silverware (ties in with the above)

Places are always open, and therefore people are always working (also ties in with above)

Notice of the level of consumerism that simply isn't present in their home country

Nobody takes time to enjoy family or life itself

Taking a look at the above things that visitors from Europe several things become apparent but a couple of things become glaringly unmistakable. So, the people all look tired... that's probably got something to do with the fact that everyone is stressed out, over-worked and, as observed, in a hurry. We eat our meals on the go, we are such a people of consumerism and instant gratification that many businesses remain open 24/7, therefore having people working hours far removed from our natural circadian rhythm. We drive vehicles that consume far and away more gasoline/diesel and oil than necessary to get us where we are going. Motorcycles aren't even what you could call mainstream, nor do they fit the typical view of the "American Dream" even though they are a much more fuel-efficient means of transportation. No, you can't take your kids to school on a motorcycle but you can sure commute back and forth to work on one. On the noticing of all the disposable items, particularly cups, forks and knives, we throw almost everything away. I realize this isn't the point the visitors were making. They were making the point that people here rarely sit down and enjoy a meal, instead they take it with them or wolf it down far too fast. My point on the observation of disposable items though is that we use something and then throw it away. We even have disposable phones! Some people trade their overly-large vehicle in for yet another overly-large one every year or two. We simply use, not enjoy. Lastly, they notice that family time and simply stopping to enjoy life is not a very high priority here in America. Even if you never visit a European country, at least take the time to research it via Internet, books or documentary and one thing will become crystal clear very quickly... people there simply don't live their lives at the break-neck speed we do here. They know how to enjoy the things that matter. I'm not trying to make them out to be some sort of Utopian society, because there is no such thing. But I do believe they live a better quality of life and definitely enjoy life on a much larger scale that most Americans do. How many old American CEOs do you know of? If you know of any, how healthy are they? How healthy (mentally as well as physically) is any CEO? How's their family life (if they even have one to speak of)?

12
HOSTILE MIND TAKEOVER

Brainwashing – a scary word. No one wants to believe that they could be brainwashed, but it happens. It happens more than you even know.

Brainwashing is known by other names too – mind abuse, coercive persuasion, and thought control. What happens, is a person or even a group of people use systematic methods to get the victim to bend or conform to things they wouldn't conform to otherwise. Think about members of a cult.

That's scary, but even scarier is the fact that advertisers have learned these dark techniques and use them regularly on the unsuspecting public.

ONLY ONE CONCLUSION

The day was long, the food supply limited, and picky eaters would prove hard to deal with. I was alone with my two sons in a remote cabin in the woods. Their father had gone out hunting and wouldn't be back for at least two days.

We were on our own with the little we had. My ten and twelve-year-old sons didn't care for much, other than fast food. I had my work cut out for me.

But how to get pre-teens to think they actually wanted to eat something they'd turned down most of their lives?

"Hey, I was reading the other day how the turkey is a superfood." I brought up.

"Turkey?" Garrett asked as he made a face. My twelve-year-old thought himself a connoisseur of not so fine foods. "If that's such a superfood, then why isn't it sold at any of the places we eat, Mom?"

"Well, grapes are a superfood and you can't get them at the places you eat either." I felt that needed to be pointed out. "And we are out here in the wilderness - twenty miles from any town. If your dad doesn't make it back for any reason, then we'll have to hoof it out of here. And the snow is only getting deeper by the day."

"Are you saying that we should build ourselves up in case we have to walk out of here, Mom?" Bryan, our ten-year-old asked.

I shrugged. "You never know. Might as well be prepared, right?"

My sons looked at each other than Garrett asked, "So, what about this turkey you read about?"

"It's a superfood. It's got protein and other vital nutrients."

"Yeah, and it's gross," Bryan said.

"Do you think that muscle building protein is gross, Bryan?" I asked.

Garret flexed his tiny bicep. "I'm strong enough."

"Are you?" I looked out the window as the snow fell outside of it. "Are you strong enough to fend off, let's say, a wolfpack?"

Both boys looked a little on the frightened side. "Nope," they said.

"Do you think that eating a superfood, like a turkey could help you fight them off if it came to it?" I asked.

Bryan nodded. "Superfood is in the name, so I would think it could help."

"And what about hunger? Walking all that way, twenty miles could deplete your energy. My bets are on that it would. Wouldn't it be best to have fueled your body with the best stuff you could so that you would have stamina much longer than if you'd eaten junk?"

Garret agreed, "Yeah, eating superfoods sounds like the best thing to do if you're faced with something like that."

"Yeah," Bryan agreed.

"So, if you had the choice to eat cheese pizza or a turkey sandwich on whole grain bread, which would you pick if you had to walk twenty miles in the snow and possibly take on a pack of wolves along the way?"

"Turkey sandwiches!" they both shouted.

"Great." I got up to go make them some. "Since we have no idea what we're in for. Do you boys think tonight's dinner should be some turkey sandwiches or that one frozen cheese pizza we've got?"

"Turkey sandwiches!" they shouted again.

And we have a winner!

THE SAME PHRASE

"My mother had a new friend over the other day and something she said just won't leave my mind," I told my husband. "And Mom has been going to meet with this little church group with this woman for over a week. Now, Mom's saying this thing a lot and I don't know if I like it."

"What is it?" he asked me.

"It seems benign. I know it does, but it's just that her friend said it over and over. And now Mom's doing it." I couldn't shake the feeling that something bad might happen if I didn't tell someone what I'd overheard.

"So, what is it, Beth?" my husband asked, growing impatient.

"The name of the man who heads up this little church group – a group who meets in the member's homes, instead of a real church – is Barney." Even saying his name gave me chills.

"And what does that have to do with what this woman and your mother have been saying?" he asked me, looking aggravated as he rubbed his temples.

"It's his name. The woman kept starting out her sentences with, Barney says. It was odd. She said things like Barney says we should all eat tuna fish. My mother asked her why and I swear to you that the woman merely shrugged and said that she didn't know. No one asks Barney why he says the things he says – that would be rude. Anyway, she went on to say that since she's added tuna to her diet, she feels great."

"That's not so bad," my husband said as he laid back in our bed. "I don't see what you're worried about."

"She said other things too. Like this, Barney said we all need to put ten dollars into the pot each time we meet. And she also said Barney, says we need to meet every other day, so we don't forget the words." I shrugged. "I don't know what she meant by that, but I didn't like it. And I didn't like what I found at Mom's today."

"What did you find at your mother's house?"

"A whole shelf in her pantry is nothing but canned tuna fish. And she's got an envelope from her bank with nothing but ten-dollar bills in it too." I just knew something wasn't right with this little church group. "And she told me that she joined that group and then she said this, Barney says we should all bring at least one new person to our group each month. Barney says when we get one hundred followers that we can buy a place where we all can live. Like a camp. We will all live in one, great big home, and we will all take care of each other for the rest of our lives."

"Great!" my husband said. "I've always worried that your mother would end up living out the remainder of her years with us. Thank goodness she found this group."

"No! I think he's a cult leader or something." I smacked him on the arm. "She said that Barney says they are all going to put all their money into one account that he'll oversee and make sure everyone is taken care of."

"I still don't see a downside," my husband said, then snuggled down and went to sleep.

TOO MANY QUESTIONS

"How would you like it if a man took your wallet, Joey?" he asked me.

"I," I couldn't say anything else as he jumped right back in.

"How would you like it if someone stole your dog, Joey? How would you like it if you stepped on a nail? How would you like it if your mom went to jail? How would you like it if I took your stuffed teddy bear? How would you like it if you couldn't ever drink water again?"

"Stop!" I screamed.

But he didn't stop. "How would you like it if popcorn were no longer available? How would you like it if there wasn't any more snow, Joey? How would you like it if I ran over your toe with my car?"

"I wouldn't like any of those things."

"So, how would you like to go to the movies with me?"

"Movies? Yeah, sure." I hadn't wanted to go anywhere with him, but I'd do anything to shut him up.

WHEN FEAR BENDS YOUR MIND

I sat at my desk in my office on the fifth floor when a strange man ran into my office, breathing hard and looking scared to death. "Thank

God, I made it." He slammed the door closed behind him, locking it. "There's a fire out there. The whole place is on fire. I'm looking for all the survivors I can find to help them." He came at me quickly, pulling me out of my chair. "You've got to get out of here."

"I don't smell any fire."

"No, it's not quite here yet. But it's coming and it's coming fast. You're going to have to jump."

"I'm on the fifth floor! I can't jump."

"You would rather burn alive?"

"I would not rather burn alive."

He pushed me to the window then opened it. The ground looked so far away. "Here you go then, time to jump."

"But," I got up on the ledge. "I don't see any smoke."

"It's billowing out the other side. Hurry, there's no time to waste." He gave me a slight push. "Jump! Now!"

And so, I did and that was when I broke my legs all because of one crazy as sin man.

ISOLATION AND BRAINWASHING

Joe grew up on a remote farm with only his grandparents around. With only the three of them, Joe knew nothing more than what he'd been told his entire life.

When I got out of the car to pick him up and take him with me to a new home, a place where he'd be safe since the death of his grandparents, he tried to run away. "No. I won't go. You're not real!"

I had another caseworker come in from behind the small house. "It's okay. We're here to help you, Joe."

"No!" the fifteen-year-old boy screamed. "There's no one else on this planet. Why would they lie to me? Why?"

Joe was the victim of grandparents who thought it best to keep the boy unaware of outside life. They'd had to raise him from an infant when his mother took off and left him at their home. She was in a cult and they wouldn't let her keep the baby she'd been pregnant with before she joined them.

I had to try to make him understand why people he loved would do such a horrible thing to him, "They did it only because they loved you, Joe. But it was all a lie. Now come with us and everything will be okay. I promise."

He fell to his knees in the dark dirt. "They promised me too, lady. They promised me too!"

BRAINWASHING IN ADVERTISING

I sat there, my toothbrush in hand and the tube of toothpaste that I'd used for years and years in the other. "Nine out of ten dentists recommend this brand, Danny. You should use it too."

"How do you know that's true?" My new boyfriend came to stand at my side. "I use the other brand and guess what?"

"What?" I asked as I began brushing my teeth.

"That commercial says that nine out of ten dentists recommend my brand too. Think you might've been brainwashed?"

Have I?

13
JOHN F. KENNEDY'S ASSASSINATION

A bit over 50 years ago, President John F. Kennedy was murdered on tour to Dallas, Texas, two years after his term. A Warren Commission inquiry concluded a retired U.S. Navy seal called Lee Harvey Oswald fired Kennedy from a local book depository; however, the unclear nature of the event contributed to a variety of possible hypotheses.

Most theories of JFK center on the notion that Oswald did not operate alone. The convoy was approaching a grassy knoll on the northern side of Elm Street when the president was struck by the bullet that killed him. Newspaper photos show that police captured three tramps hidden in a train car behind knoll soon after the attack. Since the people were found to be clean-shaven and well-fed, rumors emerged that they were agents of the CIA rather than crack heads.

The suggestion that the murder was a CIA scheme seems insane, but theories say the president's supposed statement that he wished to "cut the CIA into a thousand bits and spread it to the winds" has made him an agency priority. Many reports say that one of the hobos was E. Howard Chase, a former CIA agent who was interested in overthrowing Cuban leader Fidel Castro in the poorly-fated Bay of Pigs project.

Another theory is mafia related. But why is it that the mafia wishes JFK dead? Robert, his brother, turned on the pressure on organized crime. At the moment, Robert was the US secretary of state, and his "anti-mafia campaign" has contributed to a dramatic rise in the number of top mafia members arrested.

Another hypothesis claims that JFK was murdered because they demonstrated so considerable interest in "evil practices." There are two "crucial" pieces of evidence to support this. The first one was a letter JFK sent to the CIA asking to see classified UFO files. The other was a notice from a top CIA official stating, "We can't authorize" the president to see all the information confidential.

The underground puppet masters running the planet are easy targets for a conspiracy by JFK. The president wanted to get rid of Illuminati; it was claimed that he tried to stop the Vietnam War, a fight that yielded the lovely dividends of the "shadowy banks." JFK's efforts to "rein in" the influence of the US Treasury department have "affected" the Freemasons, sparking a lethal revolt.

Another theory blames the guy holding the black umbrella. Several sources refer to a "mysterious" individual carrying an umbrella as the motorcade of JFK passed past. The assassination day was nice and bright; no one in the crowd, but one individual, is sporting a raincoat or holding an umbrella. And he was seen exactly where someone fired the bullets.

People who claim that the CIA was responsible for the assassination of Kennedy suspect that the government actively criticized a variety of positions regarding Cuba and socialism. The hypothesis suggests that Jfk's failure to provide air cover for the unsuccessful invasion of Bay of Pigs, a plan supported by the CIA to topple Fidel Castro, prompted the CIA to remove Kennedy completely from the scene.

A similar hypothesis claims that the CIA has been collaborating with the Mob to execute Kennedy. The two groups at the time had a common purpose in overturning Castro because the Mob owned a variety of high-risk stakes in Cuban businesses that were shut down. Some claim that the operation was much less complex than a government coup, albeit undertaken by a group of disgruntled Cuban exiles who saw the attempted invasion of the Bay of Pigs as ample proof that Kennedy was unfit for president.

One hypothesis argues that in the 1964 race, Lyndon B. Johnson hated being stripped so deeply from the Presidential ballot that he was planning to have JFK killed.

This is accurate that Kennedy wanted to succeed Johnson as vice-president, according to a 1968 autobiography published by Kennedy's assistant, Evelyn Lincoln. On 19 November 1963, Kennedy told Lincoln as much — three days before he was assassinated. Many historians also claim that an assassination of Kennedy, guided by Premier Nikita Khrushchev, was carried out by a band of Soviet officers.

Ultimately, at the end of the Cuban Missile Crisis of 1962, Khrushchev was compelled to withdraw the nuclear missiles that he had installed in Cuba owing to US military attacks towards the Soviet Union.

Conspiracists say that the change inspired Khrushchev to destroy Kennedys" lobbies had been significantly destroyed prior to the towers' demise. There were no chance the jet's impact caused too extensive destruction 80 floors below.

GLOSSARY

Because Q's posts include terms you may not be familiar with, I've provided a glossary to help decode abbreviations, acronyms, symbols, names, and agencies. The decodes I've provided are not to be taken as the only possible correct ones. There are, no doubt, valid decodes

I have not considered and have not included. Some abbreviations have been confirmed by Q to have multiple meanings. As Q's mission continues, some abbreviations that have been used in one way may later be used in a different way. In such cases, the context of a particular post should be used to determine the best interpretation. The terms in this glossary are not exclusive to posts found in this book. They pertain to the entirety of Q's operation to date.

Note: names and initials are alphabetized as they appear in Q posts which is usually the first name followed by the last name.

/calmbeforethestorm/ or /CBTS/ --- An 8chan board where Q has posted messages.

/greatawakening/ or /GA/ --- A read-only board on 8chan where Q has posted.

GLOSSARY

/patriotsfight/ or /pf/ --- An 8chan board where Q has posted messages.

/pol/ --- Boards on 4chan and 8chan where Q has posted messages.

/projectdcomms/ --- A read-only board on 8kun where Q posts.

/qresearch/ --- Boards on 8chan and 8kun where anons can interact with Q.

/thestorm/ --- An 8chan board where Q has posted messages.

/_ --- A three-sided shape used by Q to illustrate the power structure of the three wealthiest and most politically influential families in the world; the Saudi royal family (removed from power in 2017) the Rothschilds, and George Soros. Q's mission involves the gradual removal of all three sides of the triangle, representing the removal of these families from power.

#FLY# --- Q uses the word FLY along with a name and pound sign (#) to indicate a person whose influence has been neutralized or a politician who has been removed from office.

[] --- Brackets indicate different things depending on the context. Q answered an Anon's inquiry by indicating that brackets signified a "kill box" but sometimes brackets are used to highlight letters that spell out a message hidden within a post, for example, [p], [r], [a], [y]. Brackets can also be used to disrupt computer programs used by opponents that search Q's posts for key words.

[F] --- Foreign

(You) --- When viewing posts on 4chan, 8chan, or 8kun, the word "you" is displayed in parenthesis to indicate that you are viewing your own post.

4-10-20 --- Initials of Donald John Trump when the numbers are replaced with the corresponding letters of the alphabet.

4chan --- An internet message board where users can post anonymously.

GLOSSARY

5 Eyes or Five Eyes or FVEY --- A multilateral intelligence-sharing alliance that includes Australia, Canada, New Zealand, the United Kingdom and the United States.

7 Dwarves --- According to the Michael Kilian article Spy vs. Spy published in 2000 by The Chicago Tribune, the CIA has seven super-computers named after the seven dwarves; Doc, Dopey, Bashful, Grumpy, Sneezy, Sleepy and Happy.

5:5 --- "Five by five" is military jargon signifying loud and clear, or understood. Radio transmissions are rated for signal clarity and strength on a scale from 1-5 with 1 being the lowest and 5 being the highest. 5:5 indicates the signal is loud and clear.

8chan --- An internet message board where users can post anonymously.

8kun --- An internet message board where users can post anonymously. Created in 2019 after 8chan was de-platformed.

A or A's --- Agency, agencies, intelligence agencies.

Alice and Wonderland --- A signature phrase that Q helped anons decode. Alice is Hillary Clinton. Wonderland is Saudi Arabia. Q says Saudi Arabia has been the source of funding for many U.S. politicians.

Alphabet --- The parent company of Google, YouTube, and others subsidiaries.

Alice --- Hillary Clinton, as she was referred to in emails from Marty Torrey (published by WikiLeaks), who went by the moniker "Hatter."

Bakers --- Slang term for anons who assemble 4chan, 8chan, or 8kun posts (crumbs) into threads (breads) for discussion.

BB --- U.S. Attorney General William (Bill) Barr.

BC --- Bill Clinton, 42nd president of the United States from 1993 to 2001.

CA --- In most cases, it refers to California, but when used in a stringer with Uranium One (U1), it refers to Canada.

GLOSSARY

C-Info --- Confidential or Classified Information.

C_A --- Central Intelligence Agency, A civilian foreign intelligence service of the U.S. federal government.

CM --- Code Monkey, the administrator who provided technical support for Q's board on 8chan, and the current administrator of 8kun.

DJT --- Donald John Trump, the 45th President of the United States. Before entering politics, he was a businessman and television personality.

Eagle --- Secret Service code name for President Bill Clinton.

Epstein Island --- Little Saint James Island, owned by Jeffrey Epstein

Fag --- Slang term for an anon. It is sometimes combined with areas of interest, i.e. biblefag, planefag, lawfag, etc.

Fake wood --- Hollywood

Fantasy Land --- A Q signature indicating a truth that is too wild for the average person to believe. Cognitive dissonance is caused by information that challenges a programmed way of thinking.

Game Theory --- The study of conflict and cooperation by opponents within a competitive game environment.

Gang of 8 --- A term used to describe the eight leaders in the United States Congress who are briefed on classified intelligence matters. It includes the leaders of both parties from the Senate and House of Representatives, and the chairs and ranking minority members of both the Senate and House Intelligence Committees.

GCHQ --- An acronym for the Government Communications Headquarters, an intelligence and security organization responsible for providing signals intelligence (SIGINT) and information to the UK government and armed forces.

Honeypot --- A scheme used to lure people into behaviors that are unethical, immoral, or illegal. Their participation can be recorded and used as leverage to control them.

GLOSSARY

HRC --- Hillary Clinton, former Secretary of State under Barack Obama. Democratic Presidential Candidate in 2016. Wife of President William Jefferson Clinton.

IRL --- In real life, as opposed to online.

JA --- Julian Assange, founder of WikiLeaks, a watchdog organization that publishes leaked documents.

Marker --- A reference in a post by Q intended to mark a topic.

Moar --- Slang term for "more" used on 4chan, 8chan, and 8kun.

Mockingbird --- Operation Mockingbird was a CIA operation where the agency recruited news reporters and their managers to disseminate propaganda for the purpose of controlling the masses.

Mueller --- Robert Mueller, former FBI Director and Special Counsel.

NSA --- National Security Agency is a signals intelligence agency within the U.S. Department of Defense. It collects and analyzes electronic signals intelligence of interest to the security of the U.S. and protects all classified and sensitive information stored on government information technology equipment. In addition, the NSA supports and contributes to the civilian use of cryptography and computer security measures.

NWO --- New World Order, sometimes referred to as a one-world government. A governmental concept where individual nations surrender their political sovereignty to the will of a centralized world governmental power.

Pain or [PAIN] --- A reference to the pending prosecution of corrupt individuals.

PG --- Pizzagate/PedoGate, an internet controversy that surfaced in 2016, where restaurant owner James Alefantis and John Podesta were accused of pedophilia.

GLOSSARY

Q Clearance --- Access to the highest level of classified information in the U.S. Department of Energy. Q suggested in his case; it refers to the highest level of access across all departments.

R's --- Republicans

RM --- Robert Mueller, Special Counsel who investigated President Donald Trump. Served as FBI Director from 2001-2013.

SAP --- Special Access Program, a security protocol used by the U.S. federal government that provides highly classified information with safeguards and access restrictions that exceed those used for regular classified information.

Sauce --- Slang term derived from the word "source." When information is provided on 4chan, 8chan, or 8kun that is not common knowledge, the one posting the information will frequently be asked to provide a source (sauce).

Snowden --- Edward Snowden, the former CIA employee and NSA contractor who stole and made public two classified NSA surveillance programs—PRISM and XKeyscore.

Snow White --- A signature by Q referring to the CIA, so named because of the Agency's seven supercomputers that are named after the seven dwarves.

The Bloody Wonderland --- Q's reference to Saudi Arabia, which was notorious in the past for its frequent use of public execution.

Unmask --- Exposing the concealed name of a U.S. person in surveillance data.

Vault 7 --- A series of documents published by WikiLeaks in 2017 that detail the capabilities of the CIA to perform electronic surveillance and cyber warfare.

Wet Works --- Slang for assassination. The term was used in the John Podesta emails published by WikiLeaks.

WH --- White House, the official residence and workplace of the President of the United States. White House is also used as a metonym for the President and his advisors.

Where we go one, we go all --- A line from the film White Squall which was based on the sinking of a school Brigantine sailing ship in 1961. The phrase "Where we go one, we go all" is a signature found in many of Q's posts.

Who performs in a circus? --- Clowns, which is a reference to the CIA; an agency also known as Clowns in America.

Wizards & Warlocks --- An internal name used by NSA employees and contractors—guardians of all electronic information.

WL --- WikiLeaks, a watchdog organization founded by Julian Assange that publishes documents leaked from various government and corporate sources.

WRWY --- We are with you.

WWG1WGA --- The abbreviation for "Where we go one, we go all," a line from the film White Squall which was based on the sinking of a school Brigantine sailing ship in 1961. The phrase "Where we go one, we go all" is a signature found in many of Q's posts.

Y --- Generally, refers to the goat head and owl symbolism, images, and icons used by the occult. It has also been used in references to former FBI Director James Come[Y] and with reference to his book, A Higher Loyalty [Y].

www.ingramcontent.com/pod-product-compliance
Lightning Source LLC
Chambersburg PA
CBHW071725020426
42333CB00017B/2395